Finding Your People

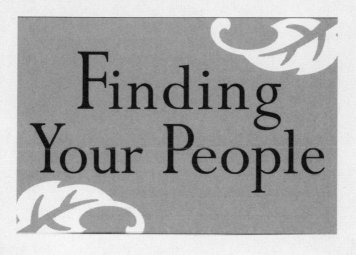

Finding Your People

*An African-American Guide to
Discovering Your Roots*

SANDRA LEE JAMISON

PERIGEE BOOKS

A Perigee Book
Published by The Berkley Publishing Group
A member of Penguin Putnam Inc.
375 Hudson Street
New York, New York 10014

First edition: February 1999

Published simultaneously in Canada.

The Penguin Putnam Inc. World Wide Web site address is
http://www.penguinputnam.com

Library of Congress Cataloging-in-Publication Data

Jamison, Sandra Lee.
    Finding your people : an African-American guide to discovering
your roots / by Sandra Lee Jamison.
        p.   cm.
    "A Perigee book."
    ISBN 0-399-52478-9
    1. Afro-Americans—Genealogy—Handbooks, manuals, etc.   I. Title.
E185.96.J28   1999
929'.1'08996073—dc21   98-42995
                                                              CIP

Printed in the United States of America
10   9   8   7   6   5   4   3

To my loving parents,
Arthur and Lois Jamison

CONTENTS

	Foreword	xi
	Introduction	1
1	Why Genealogy?	7
2	Who Are African-Americans?	17
3	How to Start?	26
4	What Am I Looking For?	44
5	What's in a Name?	56
6	Local Sources	62
7	National Sources	69
8	International Resources	92
9	Specialized Resources	104
10	Family Reunions	122
11	Methodology	126
12	Worksheets	132
	Bibliography	150
	Index	158

ACKNOWLEDGMENTS

I first wish to acknowledge the love and faithfulness of my fore-fathers, foremothers, and God who are my strength in all things. There are also many other people to thank for their early blessings and support. Rosemary L. Bray provided encouragement, kindness, and generosity that made writing this book possible. Denise L. Stinson was courageous and tenacious in representing a fledgling author. And I must resist thanking every family member, friend, acquaintance, and foe that shape my work and my life. However, there are friends and colleagues who provided family stories, proofreading, and research that was enormously helpful to this book. Special thanks to Marilyn Annan, Wanda Jones, Takashi "T. C." Curd, Denise Wilson, John Sotomayor, Tania Mayhew, Fredrick Bush, and Robert Payton for your time and thoughtfulness. Seminar leaders David A.G. Johnson, Jr., and Alene L. Smith provided skills building and direction via the Schomburg Center for Research in Black Culture and the Schomburg Corporation Genealogy Committee's workshop series. My editor, Dolores McMullan, and editorial assistant Erin Stryker have been the epitome of patience and skill in bringing focus, order, and closure to the many phases of this book. Without their guidance I would still be researching, writing, and rewriting.

I am grateful to have a sister, Sheila, who helps me maintain a balance of work and play. Thank you Mommy and Daddy for not only bringing me into this world but teaching me to ask the right questions.

FOREWORD

"So, who are your people?" the leathery faced merchant asked while bagging peppermint pillows from the candy jar and plucking dill pickles from the wooden barrel. The man's question was a cozy, southern, genteel way of getting into our business, of asking, "Who are you?" "Who are your parents?" "Who were their parents?" In a small town like Asheboro, North Carolina, there was sure to be some shared connection. This roundabout way of ascertaining what sort of family you came from—working, churchgoing, partying, or trifling, is a means of introduction still used by brown, black, and white folk alike in small communities and townships. With pigtails wiggling, my sister, Sheila, and I answered with youthful arrogance that we are the grandnieces of the Marleys on Frank Street. We went on to tell how we were kin to Edna, Dora, Lucille, Mae, Dorothy, Jean, and Fred. During those North Carolina summers spent with my parents' family in the 1960s, I learned to see myself as a link in a chain of people reaching way back. It wasn't until I grew older that I realized I had only truly explored one side of that chain—my maternal side—but knew little of my father's side.

Finding my paternal grandfather's family—a heritage and part of myself I never knew—is a challenge I undertook only recently. This book is a celebration of my success and an introduction to the nuances and challenges of researching family history for people of the African-Negro-colored-Afro-American-Black-African-American diaspora. Since I will be exploring the contrasts of Black and White family history, most often the appellation "Black" is used in this book. I choose to alternate the designations "Black" and "African-American" because I hold all of the African diaspora as significant to this work.

When I began researching my family history, I made a few false starts and took more than a few missteps. I used the wrong sources, applied bad strategy, and held unrealistic expectations. You can benefit from my newfound wisdom and learn from my mistakes. By sharing strategy and approaches to genealogical research with the Black community, I hope to constructively affect how we think of ourselves in the present. Too often I was told by well-meaning naysayers that Black genealogy couldn't be done—that there were no records of our earliest ancestors. I was surprised by the negative and defeated attitudes about tracing Black genealogy, even from friends and relatives, who told me, "Black people have no ancestry beyond slavery!" and "You can't do genealogy for Blacks because with slavery it ended," and "There's nothing worth remembering about the past." It seemed that people I spoke with just didn't want to dig up the anguish associated with Black roots. The opinion that a descendant of enslaved Africans could not trace their heritage presented an interesting challenge to the rebel researcher in me.

I learned quickly that hundreds of thousands of African-Americans are tracing their roots—with varying degrees of success.

Sourcebooks and guidebooks are plentiful in genealogical literature. There are many books on the more popular aspects of genealogy: royal lineage, British peerage, heraldry. Scottish, German, Spanish, French, and Jewish heritages are extensively documented in genealogical literature. But there are also excellent resources on the documentary history of Blacks in the Americas, and scores of organizations and associations devoted to Black genealogy. Charles Blockson's *Black Genealogy* remains a pivotal work of scholarship on this subject and is still available in libraries and bookstores. *The African American Genealogical Sourcebook,* edited by Paula K. Byers, is an extensive compendium of informational resources and Black genealogical history.

For the "tentative" and "reluctant" genealogical beginner, these sources may be more academic and scholarly than you need at first. Fascinating details about slave narratives, Blacks in the Civil War, and Abolitionist movements have been published. But even as an experienced researcher, I found these resources offered more information than I wanted at the outset of my ancestor hunt.

Using my experience as an information professional, I set out to establish which among the many types of genealogy resources available would be most useful to a beginner. I am sharing those creative shortcuts and straightforward problem-solving that can make a genealogy project possible for you.

Just as a painter prepares a surface for painting, this book will use broad strokes to smooth, sketch, and color to prepare an approach to Black genealogy. After the picture has been sketched and ordered, the reds, blues, and yellows that evoke expression, form, and likeness are placed on the surface. Though I'm mixing metaphors with the homonyms "primer" and "primer," it is what this book is—a primer. A book of broad strokes employed to simplify a complex picture.

I will interpret genealogical jargon and elaborate on the significance of planning, strategy, tenacity, and patience as components of a successful genealogical picture. Establishing clear goals at the outset of your genealogical pursuit helps you to claim the names and places of your family history. Building on these goals allows you to develop a family history that is more complete, lively, and intimate.

This book is written for those of you who have wanted to find family members or trace your family history but were not sure how to begin; were not confident that your effort would be fruitful; or did not know if the roots of the African-American were accessible or retrievable. I offer this overview to ease some of those concerns and to assure you that finding your people is not only a possibility, but almost inevitable if you take these first steps.

INTRODUCTION

Genealogy projects can be life-affirming and spirit-sustaining. Whether described as genealogical research, connecting to kinfolk, discovering your roots, tracing your ancestry, linking souls, or finding your people—a family history project usually begins with a milestone, often one that is bittersweet and meaningful.

My quest began with a funeral . . . and ended in reunion.

After she had died, I realized how little I knew about my Grandma Kate. I had never thought much about what kind of woman she was. I'd never imagined what kind of life she lived nor what dreams she had sought—fulfilled or released. I remember she liked to drink Pepsi in its bottle straight from the "fridgaire," preferred it to "Co-Cola." I remember she had a fondness for fried liver and onions, which I would never share. I remember she believed in burning loose hairs from her comb and brush "'cause if birds got hold of your hair you'd go scatterbrained."

I didn't know if her "real" name was Kate—or Katie. I knew she lived in Durham, North Carolina, most of her adult life, and I remembered her telling me that her mother smoked tobacco from a pipe and chose to seat herself on the ground rather than a chair. But

I became much more aware of how much I *didn't* know about my grandmother when she died.

I didn't know where she was born. I didn't know the name of her eccentric mother. I had no idea what her father's name was nor where he was from. I didn't know where she was born and raised: it could have been North Carolina, South Carolina, or Georgia. I didn't even know how old she was. I only knew her as Grandma Kate—my father's mother. With tears and sadness I mourned her passing: both the loss of her special love and of the life I had not thought to ask about while there was still time.

On a damp February afternoon, a couple of dozen folk stood atop an orange mound of Carolina clay to lay Grandma to rest. During and after services, strangers approached me with their eyes full of tears and sorrow. These were faces strangely familiar yet unknown to me. We stood shoulder to shoulder and shared in mourning and grief but I had no idea who most of these folk were. The names and brief introductions slipped through my memory quickly. By the time the funeral was over and mourners dispersed, I was asking myself, "How were we all brought together to this woman? How were we connected? How did Grandma bring us to this common ground?"

While rereading her obituary, I was again struck by how little I knew of Grandma Kate's life and family. Who were these people in her life? Were any of them here? I hadn't the energy to ask questions the weekend of the funeral when people were around. Later, Grandma Kate's people would become more than simply an idea brought on by her passing, but rather a way for me to reclaim what I had let slip away. The answers lay in the past. Kate's past.

At first, I didn't want to poke and pry into Grandma's past and be accused of behavior that was inappropriate, impudent, or irreverent to her memory. Childhood admonishments to "never speak ill of the deceased" and to "let the dead bury their dead" were firmly ingrained in my psyche, and inhibited my early attempts to find

Grandma's people. I remember asking questions about when did so-and-so marry and being chastised in a way that made me shut my mouth for decades. Standing firmly planted in the present and moving only forward into the future—never back—was a source of family pride and an unspoken rule. And I asked myself, "What would I gain if I delved into the past? She had been a proud, loving grandmother. What more could I need?"

Well, what I needed and wanted was to establish names and relationships to the hugs and tears that had surrounded me on that muddy burial mound. I needed to link the future, present, and past before I could move on. I needed to know more about my family.

Believing the answer to anything begins with a plan followed by action, I wrote down the questions about Grandma I wanted to answer: Who were her parents? Where are her other siblings—dead or alive? Where are their descendants? This was a wish list of sorts, and I let my curiosity run free. I knew the answers to the questions led to more questions. Each then led to more questions, which led to action, which led to the library and books. This led to frustration. As an information specialist, I quickly found books on the subject of genealogy with a Black perspective—extensive scholarly sourcebooks and bibliographies. Useful and essential to the person already involved in genealogy, but not designed for the beginning or tentative genealogist.

Exhaustive research on Black historical organizations, Black newspapers, Black bibliographies, and various specialized resources in collections and archives are available. They are impressive and well researched. Extensive lists, addresses, and phone numbers of genealogical organizations and government agencies were compiled into two-inch thick volumes. Resources relevant to the unique African-American experience were cleverly articulated and described. But as excellent as these sources were in detailing the African-American genealogical legacy, they were not useful to me at my level of interest. I was interested in genealogy but not yet passionate. I was willing to do more reading, but I was overwhelmed with the bibliographies and treatises on colored, Negro, and slave histories. I wanted to get started, but I didn't want to start with reading a 400-page treatise. So, I left the library and went home.

At home I found my help in the least likely of places—in a telephone conversation with my father. The words and memories of my father—who had always been quiet, reserved, and private about his family stories—focused my search for Grandma's people. His memories of family and "Mother" would be the most valuable nugget in my research. Daddy rattled off names and places I had never heard mentioned before. He recalled months, dates, and places. County names—Sumpter, Columbia, and Fairfield—were clearly remembered. He knew his mother was born in Fairfield County, South Carolina. He knew the names of Grandma's siblings and even knew where some had settled, lived, and died. Most importantly, he knew how to get in touch with some of them. And, of course, he knew the name of his grandfather, Henry Taylor. He had even saved an invitation to a previous Taylor family reunion that he didn't attend—a generational get-together I wasn't even aware of.

Although the flyer was years old I called the cousin who had organized the reunion. I introduced myself as Kate's granddaughter and after an exchange of pleasantries, he added my name to the mailing list. Reunions were held every other year and I had just missed one. But I was satisfied at making a contact. Before the next reunion, I wanted to have more information on my great-grandfather Henry Taylor. I made up a chart with Grandma's information to make the relations clear in my head. My parents were both from small families, leaving me with just a few cousins. So, the prospect of meeting with a large family was intimidating. I had scant idea of how first, second, and third cousins were related!

Knowing that genealogy courses were given by the New York Public Library at the Schomburg Center for Research in Black Culture, I signed up for a workshop. There I learned about resources and strategy. I learned what questions to pose first about my grand-mother before setting out "to find her people." I learned about using various research tools and their advantages. Speakers were brought in to discuss Black migration in America and genealogical research methods. Most importantly, I met ordinary people who had discovered their roots as far back as two and three generations into slavery.

Some people in the workshop were more experienced than others but all were eager to share with me their successes and frustrations. Since I came prepared with names, approximate ages, and counties of residence for my relatives, I was directed to the appropriate census microfilm to scan for an individual family record. Knowing that my grandmother was in her late 80s when she died, I figured her family would show up as a listing in the 1900 census.

Bingo! After a few hours searching, on my first day at the census microfilm I found great-grandfather Henry Taylor. After Henry, his wife Maranda was listed, and then their children were listed from oldest to youngest. On the last line, indicated with the fraction ½ (for one out of 12 months old), was the youngest child, Kate Taylor! She was the last of seven children listed for Henry and Maranda. Had she been born one month or one year later she would have missed that census. It felt as if she had been born just at the right time for me to find her here. Everything my father told me was confirmed—ninety-five years later. It gave me chills. I was viewing a "record" made in the presence of my great-grandfather and infant grandmother. And I now had a document that I could use to further my research. Furthermore, there were the names of the other uncles and aunts my father remembered. But then there were all those *other* names.

A year later, when the date for the Taylor family reunion came it seemed everything was working against me getting there. Getting time off from my new job was difficult. And my plane was delayed for four hours. Nevertheless, family greeted me and a host of cousins stayed up to welcome me in the hotel lobby. I was feted with warm smiles, fruit salad, and iced tea. The highlight of the day was receiving the gift of my own family tee-shirt decorated with a genealogy chart. The same names I had gathered from my census document were among the other names linked in a purple cotton emblem with the family motto: "Taylor-made." I was one of a half dozen of the late Henry Taylor's other great-granddaughters who had made it to the reunion and homecoming. I had achieved my goal of finding my people before it was too late to make that connection.

Ultimately, making a connection to family is a great gift you can give yourself. Meeting my cousins and great aunts and uncles for the first time and hearing their accounts of the family's legacy of survival and success gave me a personal sense of pride, optimism, fulfillment, and completeness. It was then that the call for this book came to me, to help others from the African diaspora make the connections linking their present with their past; to find *their* "grandma's people."

1

WHY GENEALOGY?

HOW OLD IS GENEALOGY?

"Genealogy," as defined in the third edition of *The Shorter Oxford English Dictionary,* is an "account of a person's descent from an ancestor or ancestors, by enumeration of the intermediate ancestors; a pedigree . . . family stock . . . the investigation of pedigrees as a branch of study or knowledge." Taking root in shared communities, genealogy reveals shared history. Tribal unity, social cohesion, and individual identity are forged in shared history. Tales of "belonging to" and "beget from" are common in many if not all cultures.

Nations and races of people establish "origin myths," answering the questions "How did I (we) get here?" "Who are we?" "Who am I?" These myths often center on a common ancestor and encourage a shared identity. The stories survive in the altars, artifacts, customs, and religious beliefs of ancient and contemporary civilizations. Tartans, tattoos, hairdress, appellations, scarification, and holy writ all link family tribes, nations, and clans through generations. Genealogical grouping is mankind's way of distinguishing you and us from them.

There are societies that trace lineage through the mother (matrilineal) and some that trace lineage through the father (patrilineal). It is the patrilineal model that dominates in America and most of the modern world. Many African and South American societies trace family through the mother's bloodline.

England's 16th-century landowners persistently pursued scientific methods for tracing familial descent. English genealogy was territorial and proprietary in nature. Family connections were an early means to facilitate the transfer of responsibilities for land, position, and power. Transfers of land also provided a method of maintaining religious cohesion and tradition—doing things the way their fathers had done before. An entire history and mythology about kings and queens, dukes and countesses, legitimate and illegitimate heirs, chivalry and honor, cowardice and shame became a part of their heritage.

AMERICAN FASCINATION

The United States is a relatively young country, at just over two hundred years old. In comparison, countries in Asia, Europe, and Africa have histories that span thousands of years. There is evidence of Native American people, including the "Indian" cultures of Central and South America, as far back as 10,000 B.C. The European exploration of America began with the Norsemen and Vikings in the Middle Ages. Later, Spain led the rest of Europe to explore and colonize America. By the 1700s, immigration to the New World included Italians, Greeks, Turks, Irish-Catholics, Russians, Slavs, Jews, and Africans. America's heritage is a mix of ethnic and racial legacies. As a country largely made up of immigrants, Americans reaching back for their roots need to look in many directions.

Uncountable numbers of Americans participate in amateur and professional genealogy. According to a survey, over 100 million Americans have already started tracing their family history, and another three million are interested in their genealogy. The National Genealogical Society cites genealogy as the third most popular hobby in the United States, behind coin and stamp collecting. In the past, making ancestral connections to exotic parts of the world, periods of history, and famous lineages had been largely a pursuit of White affluent European-Americans, but this is no longer true. Now, Americans are more likely to embrace the discovery that they are descendants of humble people who left a continent or country to forge a new identity. Americans have a modern sense of pride in their immigrant origins.

Why Everyone Should Know Their Genealogy

Genealogy is a blood inheritance. Both literally and figuratively we exist because of the lives and challenges of the people who were here before us. Every bloodline has some good and some bad. And every genealogy history is a physical and spiritual foundation.

There are character-building benefits in drawing a connection to something larger than yourself. All members of a family can benefit and participate in family history building, since genealogical pursuits can advance in stages of interest and growth. Children can grow in their knowledge of history, and gain a healthy respect for their communities and their family. Adolescent questions and probes can be directed to ancestral detective work; the collecting of stories and artifacts and evidence of the past could even become a teenager's delight. Planning and executing a family reunion is an ideal young adult project, helping to create a legacy of pride and history. Adults and elders fuel the family network with new stories and history. A place of honor blooms as a family relearns its history and honors its people.

Genealogical research adds a satisfying texture and significance to our presence in history, and it places that history in perspective. Robert Caroon, president of the Connecticut Genealogical Society, in *The New York Times,* said that "[Genealogy] places you and your family into the historical context, and it makes [history] much more interesting."

There is even medical knowledge to be gleaned from an ancestor's life. Called a genogram, a medical pedigree is built on finding the ages, causes of death, types of illness, age of onset, and related data for detecting illness and disease. Genetic roots can be established for such conditions as cancer, heart disease, and psychological traits and tendencies. Identifying patterns of family disease has become a specialty of genealogy in and of itself, and can be a life saver.

WHY BLACK GENEALOGY?

"And, who do you think you are?"

As a little brown girl—which *is* what my birth certificate says, "brown"—I heard this taunt over and over and thought it was strange. I grew up in the Ocean-Hill Brownsville section of Brooklyn in the 1960s. Sitting, listening, and watching I learned from my elders—neighbors, friends, and family—the history of my origins. They were modest stories about freed slaves, self-taught craftsmen, landowners, house builders, taxpayers, beauticians, domestics, clergy, and teachers, but taken together, they were an informal education. Stories about building homes, constructing churches, pooling money, and acquiring land were already a part of my world. I learned about the progress and accomplishments of real people and by their example I learned that progress and accomplishment were in my grasp.

My community of elders enveloped me in memories rich in contrast and spirit: New York reminiscences of sidewalk games, big city shops, street singers, and all the passion and pageantry that a Brooklyn Baptist church could muster; North Carolina summers echoing kindness and community, hard work and discipline, sweat and gospel. I learned firsthand how "my people" made ironic triumphs. Mine was a legacy of a people making lasting beauty and dignity in the midst of the horror and brutality of slavery and racism. I learned faith and courage. Family taught me whose I was—and who I am.

Family stories and family pride are rooted in the past, and ever growing in the present. With the passion and enthusiasm of a child coming of age during the Civil Rights and Black Power movements, I embraced Swahili, dashikis, and Afros as affirmations of African pride and beauty. However, I also embraced the achievements of the "African-nigra-Negro-colored-black-Black-Afro-American" experience that defined Absalom Jones, Nat Turner, Benjamin Banneker, Sojourner Truth, Mary McCloud Bethune, Marian Anderson, and Ray Charles. I read about and experienced the Black is Beautiful movement that instilled pride in native African progeny and culture. And I claimed it.

As a student, I had learned early that Black people were descendants of Ethiopian royalty and Egyptian pharaohs. To me, Black people were just once or twice removed from the Queen of Sheba and the goddess Isis. In my youthful imagination, Nefertiti, Hannibal, and Cleopatra were much more than entries in the encyclopedia, they were melanin-enhanced cousins. This seemed entirely plausible because I knew that I was a descendant of survivors and achievers who had overcome the wretchedness of slavery and the insult of second class citizenship.

This is why, to the schoolyard challenge, "Who do you think you are?" I imagined answering, "I am the daughter of Arthur who is the husband of Lois who is the daughter of Edna. . . ." Perhaps wisely, I kept silent.

In 1977, my childhood daydreams of making a connection between ancient Africa and modern America were given context. That year, for eight consecutive nights, Alex Haley's 1976 historical novelization, *Roots,* was televised. The broadcast, watched by an estimated 130 million households, broke audience records. And it brought another dimension of Black America into American households. *Roots* triggered the movement that came to be known as African-American history.

Seemingly overnight, the appellation "African" lost its stigma—among Whites and Blacks alike! "The African" was embodied in Kunta Kinte. His Gambian family, his kidnaping, his agonizing journey on a slave ship, his torture, his triumph, and his pride were rich symbolism of things African. Kunta Kinte and his kinfolk—Kizzy, Chicken George, and Queen—gave Black Americans new identification and pride in their African roots. And this pride continues to grow.

Roots helped to lift the cloud of shame over slavery. Elders began to talk about the experience and legacy of slavery in their families. Slavery became an acknowledged part of the Black experience. *Roots* provided new context for African-American history and a viable model for genealogical research. Our ancestors were no longer "slaves" but "enslaved Africans." Because of *Roots,* slavery was talked about and recognized as an atrocity and an assault on innocent people.

Slavery, as an issue, comes up again and again throughout the Black genealogy experience. Angry, ambivalent, confused, and erroneous ideas about the lives of the early African-Americans in the United States had hindered Blacks researching their family trees. *Roots* helped to illustrate the dignity, courage, and love within Black families and made those stories emotionally, intellectually, and visually desirable. Family stories about overcoming barriers, being denied rights, and being treated as less than human are rooted in the slavery legacy. These memories are painful for many, since they speak of Black inferiority. But the *Roots* model gave the descendants of displaced Africans new associations. There were stories of farmers, tradesmen, mothers, children, entrepreneurs, and achievements both humble and honorable.

Black American history remains largely untapped in America's story. These Black and White family legends can be woven into the fabric of the American psyche and American history one thread—one story—at a time. The personal triumphs and everyday sacrifices of hundreds of thousands of individuals are part of everyone's heritage. The simple, steady success stories of everyday Black people—your people—are rich and significant, yet they probably remain unclaimed and unknown. Black people can gather new strength and new vision from the contributions of our common kinfolk. We can identify new heroes and heroines. We can provide balance to the negative images that still dominate American media. I believe we can undermine the negative with the positive, spirit enhancing, loving, and compassionate stories that are ours to tell.

As a youngster, I delighted in the unknown history of Black folk. I fancied myself an amateur anthropologist, and I rejoiced as ancient relics in the Sudan were recovered to establish the Black African origins of ancient Egypt and made the word "Nubian" popular. I reveled in the discovery of early African burial grounds in America, which contradicted the heathen and "unchurched" stereotype of the enslaved African. Analyzing and understanding the survival tactics of the African community could probably teach us something today. Our Black ancestors participated in midwifery and herbalism to tend to their own sick and infirmed. It was not uncommon to hear of a mother breaking an arm or leg of her child to "damage" him and prevent him from being sold. Early in their freedom, Blacks purchased hundreds of acres of land and slaves. Much is made about Black slave owners, but these slave and master relationships were often different from that of White slave owners. They were often familial relationships complicated by the social and economic structure of the times. Blacks established towns and cities. The Black occupations during Reconstruction ran the gamut of government, science, culinary, cultural, spiritual, and recreational achievements. However, that legacy is remote and doubtful in the collective mind of the American public. Black participation in genealogy makes the rediscovery of Black achievement vivid and personal. The stories of African survival in American and African culture are available to be reclaimed.

But slavery is neither the end nor the beginning of our history. Every family has stories of which they're proud. Stories of achievement and loss, faith and despair, survival and suffering. When starting a family history project, you can select which path along your ancestral trail to follow. You can make the effort to document the lineage prior to and leading up to the life of an enslaved ancestor—perhaps even back to Africa. Or, if you are uncomfortable with the slave experience, do your ancestor hunting after the Emancipation Proclamation. African-Americans should invest time in genealogy now. A history in which we can take much pride is in danger of slipping away. Older relatives are the keepers of many of the stories we need to reclaim. They are the repositories of the information you need to get a family history project started. With their deaths, these wise ones will take irreplaceable knowledge with them. Much of this wisdom forms the heart of family stories.

IF YOU DON'T TELL YOUR STORY, WHO WILL?

The history of the African-American experience, in literature, journalism, letters, and archival information, has often been inaccurate, incomplete, and replete with racist and dehumanizing language. And much of this printed information is fragile and vulnerable to destruction and loss. These records provide hard evidence and clues to the life and times of our forbears. Choosing to do a genealogy project now can assure that the information is available to future generations. Most importantly, your project can contribute a new positive history. Americans of African descent should learn and claim their personal stories and history to challenge the ignorance about Black history. Our collective stories of Black struggle, sacrifice, and success are wonderful. Perhaps we sometimes believe the worst about ourselves because we stopped sharing such stories.

WHO DOES GENEALOGY?

In 1977, the same year *Roots* was televised, the Afro-American Historical and Genealogical Society was founded in Washington, DC. It was also the year the African-American History Association in Atlanta, GA, was founded. In the decades that followed, hundreds of Blacks—now African-Americans—began researching their lineages with the help of such organizations.

African-Americans participate in genealogy with the same zeal as their European-American counterparts. A growing African-American middle-class overcame the obstacles of embarrassment, access, cost, and time that made genealogy prohibitive to past generations. The African-American History Association has over 300 members nationwide and the Afro-American Historical and Genealogical Society has over 1,000 individual and institutional members. There are dozens of formal and informal genealogical groups and clubs meeting in almost every state.

The cost of doing genealogy varies from situation to situation. Some people doing genealogy travel and visit ancestral homesteads, or use state of the art electronic and computerized resources. But some genealogists work with a notebook and pencil. The expenses incurred usually include the costs of telephone calls, postage, photo-duplication services (usually less than $10 per document), photocopying from microfilm (ranging from $.05 to $.50 per page), and reading materials (from free library loans to $.50 pamphlets to $100 sourcebooks). These fees for services and information are not insurmountable, and the Black working-class and middle-class have begun researching their pedigree in earnest.

Uncovering family history and making ancestral connections is as time-consuming as it is challenging. It is often tedious, and it is often fruitless for months at a time. You must take on the role of detective. Ask questions. Take notes. Follow-up on clues. Record and protect the evidence you gather. Be patient.

A knowledge of your family history will strengthen your self-esteem and confidence, especially knowing that your family survived difficult times. This knowledge is valuable to both the old and the young. Aggressively pursue genealogy activities involving young people. Pedigree sleuthing can provide guidance and meaning to a child or teenager. Knowing the details about himself and his family can create a special resonance in the African-American youth, who still must fight negative stereotypes.

There is nothing new in youth struggling to define themselves for themselves, but too many of our Black youth are struggling without personal knowledge of their deep ancestral roots. Even though, as a child, I didn't know both my maternal and paternal lineages of Jamisons, Marleys, and Taylors, I grew up confident about my place in the Divine Order and "who my people were." So, "Who do you think *you* are?"

2

WHO ARE AFRICAN-AMERICANS?

In modern history books, the African presence often begins with colonial American slavery. Despite evidence and knowledge of the very civilized peoples of Africa, the greatness and glory of African culture has not yet become a part of everyday vocabulary. African history is a much older and much nobler history than standard reference books and resources represent. There are esoteric studies of biblical history, ancient archaeology, Greco-Roman antiquity, and "primitivism" about Africa. The ancient histories of Herodotus and early explorers describe centuries old relationships with "black Africa" and her people.

Before the 17th century, the African was not perceived as subhuman and inferior. Great African kingdoms—Mali, Kush, Dahomey, Timbuktu, Songhay, and Egypt—were prominent in world history and influence. These nations traded in gold, salt, and spices. European merchants and voyagers interacted and traded with African peoples without prejudice. The African presence in recorded history was rich and varied. It was a huge continent with many lands, regions, and countries. Many characters in the Judaeo-Christian texts have been identified as Black; among them Ham, Simeon the Crimean, and the Queen of Sheba. Greco-Roman histories, sciences, and philosophies cite great

African kingdoms. The unrecorded history of Africa as the mother of civilization is rich. Sadly, this knowledge is often kept in the realm of scholars, academics, and scientists.

A peek at just a few prominent African kingdoms reveals much in the African legacy of which to be proud. Ethiopia, an African kingdom dating back to 1000 B.C., was founded by the descendants of the biblical Solomon and has a rich economic, social, and philosophical history. The kingdom of Aksum and the dynasty of Haile Selassie emanate from Ethiopian roots. Benin, settled in the early 12th century, produced the great warrior peoples of Dahomey. This kingdom flourished in the 14th century and continued to dominate its region in the trade of ivory, pepper, cloth, and slaves to Europeans. The artisans of Benin are among the earliest innovators of metalworking in bronze and iron.

Egypt has been established as one of the oldest and most fascinating civilizations in the world. Yet many historical accounts resist even placing this ancient kingdom within the African continent! Egypt's artistic, religious, philosophical, political, and social influences dominate much of ancient history. To assert that Egypt was a kingdom of African/ Black/Negroid peoples still angers many scholars and theorists. However, it has been confirmed that the origins of pre-dynastic Egypt lay in the Sudanese region—"Black" Africa.

Ashanti—the ancient kingdom of present day Ghana—was noted for its goldwork and trade. The magnificence of Ashanti crafts and skill made their wares valuable in trade and commerce. The Ashanti presence continues to dominate the central Ghanian region.

The triumphs and glory of modern and ancient Africa are being revisited and rewritten. Constructive assessments and descriptions of African trade, religion, society, and politics are becoming easier to find in libraries and bookstores.

In ancient times, slavery and indentured servitude were common in continental Europe, Asia, and Africa. Slavery was a byproduct of war: Losers in battle were conquered and enslaved. However, the westward transport of African slaves by Europeans was a new kind of slavery known as chattel slavery. Harsher and more inhumane than "traditional" slavery, it virtually eliminated the African slaves' humanity. Africans were not adequately prepared to protect against or react to the atrocity of White slavers exporting their people westward over the Atlantic Ocean to America—the Middle Passage. One must also come to accept the failure of Africa and Africans in their underestimation of European colonialization. This "new" slave trade commanded a rationalization of a higher order—racial inferiority. To justify their barbarism and peddling, colonial slavers developed racist distortions of Black inferiority. Former African allies were now enslaved as property. This racist revisionism would cloud and eliminate the achievements and history of African people for generations. The African slave trade and colonialism disrupted and distorted the perception of the African.

AFRICAN DIASPORA

African history and African-American history doesn't start in Jamestown, Virginia in 1619. It doesn't even begin with the Black explorers who accompanied Christopher Columbus in 1492. It begins in Africa and the birth of civilization. There is no shame but much honor in bearing an African pedigree. It is a heritage that moves into the kingdoms of Benin, Ashanti, Ethiopia, and Egypt. Black Africans can be found in the earliest civilizations of Europe, Asia, Canada, Australia, and North, Central, and South America. This is important to remember when you try to locate African ancestors.

AMERICAN HISTORY

Much of what early Americans, and even African-Americans, knew of Africa came from popular culture. Early America was populated by large pockets of rural, agrarian, and illiterate masses. In storytelling, the dark-skinned African was depicted as an ungodly, primitive, uncivilized, and brainless savage. These lies fostered an evil and destructive relationship between Blacks and Whites. Today, slavery's legacy of White supremacy, Black inferiority, pain, brutality, and anguish continues to fracture the American psyche, manifesting itself in anger, prejudice, violence, and death. Unfortunately, these are stepping-stones in the African-American's racial history that the genealogist must be prepared to retrace—and reexperience. It is a painful legacy that still lies close to the hearts and bloodlines today. It is a place to which some would rather not return. Researching personal pedigrees back to slavery can be heartrending and difficult: You may find ancestors listed in plantation bills of sale along with barnyard animals, lumber purchases, and food rations. But such documentation—which also includes ships' cargo lists, captain's logs, journals, bills of sale, and plantation diaries—can be used to connect enslaved Africans to contemporary African-American bloodlines. It is not easy, but reclaiming those personal histories lost in dusty archives and vaults adds to your knowledge of your ancestors and their time. The past, present, and future are all touched in us here and now.

Some people will not want to attempt reviewing this history. But it is not necessary to focus your genealogy research in "going back to Africa." There are hundreds of dignified, eloquent, proud stories of ancestry that lie between that first African-American ancestor and yourself, including the post-Emancipation stories of farmers, laborers, educators, artists, craftsmen, homemakers, and professionals. Slavery is not a part of every African-American's legacy. Africans immigrated to this country just as Europeans did at Ellis Island.

Recreating personal genealogies can create a new understanding of the bittersweet legacy of the Ethiopian-African-Negro-colored-black-African-American diaspora. And in the last thirty years, Blacks have begun to proudly claim their African legacy and proclaim themselves African-Americans. The accomplishments, achievements, protests, and striving of the African in the New World has been given new significance.

African-Americans tracing their roots should prepare themselves for dealing with the fact that many of the resources needed to identify their genealogy will treat their ancestors as chattel. There is no telling how one will react to finding one's ancestor listed in a plantation diary or auctioneer's journal. There is frustration that these African ancestors—unlike most European immigrants—were neither enumerated on passenger lists, nor granted the privileges of citizenship upon their arrival. But remember that not every Black person in colonial America was enslaved. Focusing your research on slaves is shortsighted. In 1619, indentured servants, not slaves, were the first Blacks to arrive in America. The documentary legacy of these soldiers, craftsmen, freemen, and property holders is still not explored as fully as that of the Black slave. Indentured servants were listed in early 17th-century censuses records. They were free. Look for contracts, emancipation papers, and records of property exchanges in personal archives for clues to your ancestors' origins. Many Blacks managed to purchase their freedom and that of their families. These emancipation records were prized possessions and were often among estate records of the freeman and the slaveowner. And many more can be found in county, state, national, and private genealogical collections.

From birth to death, it is nearly impossible for someone to leave no record of his or her life. Incidental, oral, or written records are the footprints genealogists follow to reinvent an ancestor's life. Relationship stories, diaries, journals, associations, artifacts, and graveyards are a part of an ancestor's legacy.

Don't overlook the African-American presence in the central, midwest, and western states when tracing your ancestors. Achievements of Black cowboys, ranchers, and farmers are a part of rarely discussed western contribution to American history.

MISCEGENATION

Mixed race ancestry is a fact of American life. In spite of the legalistic and societal restrictions on interracial sexual unions, they occurred. There are very few "pure bloods" in American family history. As the American frontier expanded, African-American, European-American, and Native-American bloodlines invariably crossed. The genealogist should prepare for these revelations. First, prepare for any shock or discomfort with the events surrounding interracial sexual relations, which could include rape or romance. But mixed racial heritage, miscegenation, is a fact of American genealogy. Frontiersmen and settlers, including Canadian, Irish, French, and Germans, openly mixed with Native-Americans and African-Americans. Geneticist Dr. Luigi Cavalli-Sforza speculates in his book *The History and Geography of Human Genes* that 80 percent of African-Americans have White ancestry. He goes on to state that 90 percent of Whites have Black ancestry. Such statements are argued and debated, but it's clear that our American ancestors are a fairly mixed up race.

Sexual relations between slaves and their masters were not uncommon. White men deemed it their right to have sexual access to enslaved Black women, and any progeny born of such unions would only increase the masters' labor pool. It was not unusual to find mention of these children in the wills or diaries of the master or mistress. You will even find rare stories of genuine interracial affection and love between Blacks and Whites. The descendants of Thomas Woodson trace their lineage to Sally Hemings. Hemings was the mistress of slave owner and third president of the United States Thomas Jefferson. The stories of illicit and taboo relations between Jefferson and his slave mistress "Black Sal," as she was called, are still the subject of ridicule and rumor. Sally Hemings was bound to Jefferson as a slave and bore several biracial children. The descendants of her line, including Thomas Woodson, number nearly 1,400.

Perhaps one of the most painful survivals of Black and White miscegenation is the practice of "passing." Passing is both a form of racial self-hate and social survival. Fair complected, mixed race Blacks were able to gain access to White communities and sidestep the racism and ostracism endured by their darker skinned brothers and sisters. Sometimes this side step was taken to gain a temporary advantage. And there are others who passed right out of the Black community. In effect, they became White. America's legacy of racial intolerance made passing as White an attractive alternative to some of our ancestors. If you know you have White ancestry and a mixed lineage, you may find a pointer to a lost family branch. Gaps in a family pedigree, where it seems a whole family disappeared, may be evidence of a branch or individual crossing into another racial group. In her memoir, *The Sweeter the Juice,* Shirley Taylor Haizlip recounts how she found her mother's full blood sister, who had been raised to believe she was White when the family had been separated after the death of the mother.

America's racial obsession makes for certain unique approaches to searching for a Black ancestor. Because divisions and distinctions were made about race, unique records and documents are available for Black genealogy. At different times in American history, there were different restrictions and circumstances to which Blacks were subjected. For example, during the Civil War, Blacks who served in the Union Army were granted freeman status. These men were given manumission papers issued by slaveowners. These papers, a valuable asset of the freed slave, were often passed down to his heirs and estate. Various post-Civil War movements, such as Marcus Garvey's Universal Negro Improvement Association, were joined by thousands of Blacks, maybe one of your ancestors. The Abolitionist movement left a poignant and damning legacy documentary about slavery. Diaries and journals provide glimpses into this White and Black collaboration. Social, civic, economic, and political gains made by African-Americans during Reconstruction (1865–1877) are only recently becoming widely known. Every aspect of American history was occupied by Blacks, as inventors, patent holders, cowboys, sharecroppers, farmers, businessmen, saloon keepers, prostitutes, politicians, and clergy.

LEGACY OF THE CARIBBEAN

The diaspora of Latino, African-American, and Afro-Latino populations in the Americas occurred because of the explorations and invasions of the European Portuguese, Spaniards, and Italians. Christopher Columbus made three significant voyages to the Americas. On the first, he established the colony of San Salvador. Columbus's second voyage claimed the island of Hispaniola, present day Haiti and the Dominican Republic. On his third voyage, Columbus reached the tip of South America.

Central, Middle, and South America were way stations for slavers. The contemporary multiracial and multicultural populations of Latin America and the Caribbean are the result of Spanish, Portuguese, French, and British slave trade and fraternization. In 1500, Pedro Cabral settled along the South American coasts. And it was in Brazil that Portuguese and Spanish invaders introduced the first forms of chattel slavery to the Americas.

A triangular trade route began at the English ports, moved on to Africa, then to the Americas and back to Europe. European goods were exported to Africa in exchange for slaves. African slaves were traded throughout the Americas—North, Central, South, and the islands—in exchange for plantation goods to be returned to England. For 200 years, brutal slave plantations, called *ecomiendas,* were established to develop a lucrative agricultural economy in the islands of Central and South America. The native populations of "Indians"—Aztecs and Mayans—were unable to overpower their captors and the brutal slave labor and exposure to disease brought by Whites killed many of them. As the slave population declined, slave hunters went further inland to replenish the slave population. This population also died. A pattern of devastation and miscegenation swelled throughout the Americas. Mestizo (mixed race) slave uprisings and escapes became so problematic that a new Black African slave trade was created. "Los Negroes," supplied by Portuguese and Spanish slavers, were brought to an alien land and made a part of its slave culture. The Black Africans were conditioned to believe that they were totally dependent on their masters. The slavers worked to keep Blacks and mixed races divided and suspicious. This was part of the "seasoning" of slaves. But by the 1700s, the islands of the Americas were experiencing major uprisings. In Cuba, Haiti, and Puerto Rico, militant Afro-Latino alliances worked to make the islands independent.

ESTIMATED ORIGINS OF SLAVES SHIPPED TO NORTH AMERICA
DURING THE SLAVE TRADE (UP TO 1808)

Nigeria	24%
Angola	24%
Ghana	16%
Senegal/Gambia	13%
Guinea-Bisseau	11%
Sierre Leone	6%
Other	6%
	100%

(Source: *Africa Is Not a Country, It's a Continent*)

Although documentation of transactions in the African slave trade are available, they are often in uncataloged and private estate libraries and collections, so they can be difficult to locate. If you do find a collection of documents, regard them carefully because slavers were not always diligent recordkeepers. Borders and nations changed, and geographic or tribal names recorded for African principalities may not be the proper name of the indigenous people. And because slaves from certain regions brought better prices, slavers often lied about a slaves origins. However, such records can be used in corroboration with supporting documents and often provide the kind of breakthrough that can connect you to ancestors in Africa.

3

How to Start?

Support

Begin your genealogy project by identifying a network of people who can support you. There are hundreds of genealogical associations in America—both general interest associations and associations specifically for African-Americans. You may decide to join one or both. Why join? Mostly because you're going to need help. A genealogy project is a collaborative effort and requires the cooperation of many individuals. Joining a society will connect you with people who share your interest and goals. The range of membership runs the gamut of amateur to professional, passionate devotee to weekend dabbler. The group's newsletters and journals will keep you apprised of new resources and tactics. Meetings will provide fellowship and keep your project alive—you'll get tips and learn from your associates' successes and mistakes. Membership will also help you do your research faster, avoid common mistakes, and learn the basics—you will build a network of encouragement for yourself, because even family members' enthusiasm will dwindle in the pursuit of family history. And telling someone about what you're going to do in your genealogy work and then facing them at the next meeting can be a great motivator.

Although the task of putting together a genealogical puzzle is a communal effort, the work of the genealogist is often solitary. Camaraderie with other genealogists and researchers is an invaluable help. Your successes can be even more thrilling and your disappointments more bearable when they are shared with like-minded individuals.

Membership often includes a fee (usually ranging from $10 to $50), but before rejecting membership as too expensive you should factor in the savings it can provide. Most associations make their resources and collections available to members, including discounts on books, magazine subscriptions and discounted access to electronic databases.

In many respects, the beginning of a genealogy project is essentially the same for Blacks and Whites. However, an African-American genealogy association can better help you through the unique challenges of Black genealogy, since they are usually equipped with specialized genealogy publications, workshops, and resource collections. These materials will give you inspiration, guidance, and support. Maintaining a connection with Blacks involved in genealogy could prove a veritable lifeline.

Prominent among the societies you should consider writing for brochures and membership information are:

The National Genealogical Society
Arlington, VA 22207-2399
(703) 525-0050
http://www.ngsgenealogy.org

As one of the oldest genealogical societies in the country (founded in 1903), its membership and resources are extensive and comprehensive. There are individuals, groups, and chapters located throughout the country dedicated to African-American history within the organization.

The Afro-American Historical and Genealogical Society
PO Box 73086, Washington, DC 20056
(202) 234-5350
Founded in 1977, Although the society provides for and encourages membership by individuals, its emphasis is on scholarly research for publication.

The African-American History Association
PO Box 115268, Atlanta, GA 30310
(404) 344-7405
This association conducts programs and tours and encourages individuals pursuing genealogy to contact them.

Contacting these organizations will help you determine which one has goals, resources, and activities that will be most helpful to your genealogical pursuit.

Getting in touch with organizations by letter will also help you sharpen your letter writing and telephone skills. And since there will be a lot of letter writing in your future—much of genealogy can be done without leaving home—why not start honing those skills now? It's good practice to start asking for what you want and seeing if what you get is what you needed! Knowing what's available and being able to clearly explain what it is you want is foremost in your strategy. When writing letters, keep the language simple. State the nature of your inquiry right up front—who you are, what you are doing, and how the recipient can help you. If you are sending background information or a biographical sketch of a subject, include it at the end of the communication or on a separate sheet. To help expedite replies, include Self-Addressed Stamped Envelopes (SASEs) at all times. Affix postage for at least two pounds. If for any reason you cannot type your correspondence, make sure your writing is legible, and never mail the original documents.

It's in Your Hands

"Behold, the only thing greater than yourself!" says "Papa," as he raises his baby to the stars in *Roots*. In genealogy, you are the center of this universe. While awaiting your membership application, start gathering what you know. It begins with you.

The pedigree chart is what most people visualize when they think of genealogy—an extended list of branches with names, dates, and relationships. The word "pedigree" is taken from a Middle English and Latin derivation of "pe de grue," meaning "foot of the crane," because of the physical resemblance of the crane's foot with the successive lines in a genealogy chart.

Begin to fill out a pedigree chart. Make several copies of the chart provided on page 31. This is one of the simplest genealogy forms to work with. Don't just fill in your birthdate. Fill in the place of birth (including county). Next fill in your parents' names. Do you know their birth, death, and marriage dates? Do you know in what county they were born? If you have that information, include it. If you don't know it, you may have identified your first set of genealogy inquiries. Yet, you still may be able to advance to the next generation. With a pedigree chart you can easily see the generations. This chart has room for five generations—each column of parents is a generation. Do you know the names of your grandparents? Can you complete their pedigree lines—birth, death, and marriage dates? And who were their parents? Do you know the full names of your great-grandparents? Each of us has eight great-grandparents. Can you list yours? This is your next project: Compile as complete a list of your great-grandparents as you are able. This fourth generation is where many people's genealogical knowledge ends—and the challenge begins.

Family pedigree charts should be filled out as thoroughly as possible. There is a traditional numbering/filing system built into the pedigree chart tradition. You are the first generation and the first entry—number 1. All proceeding entries are recorded and numbered—men on the upper register (all men will be even numbered) and women on the lower register (all female relatives will be odd numbered). For example, your father is number 2, your mother is number 3. Now place a copy of your birth certificate in a folder marked with your name and the number 1. The birth certificate would also be labelled with the number 1. The numbers assigned in a family pedigree are not just head counts but a filing aide. Folders, files, and documents can be labeled 1, 2, 3, etc. Then, at a glance, you know the sex and generational relations from a pedigree chart. You may be surprised how many generations you can advance just from this simple exercise.

If, you are not able to complete such a chart, don't fret. Here is where you begin scouting those stepping-stones. The first pieces of your family framework will be provided by interviews with your oldest family members—the family elders.

Begin with your birth certificate. How would you go about substantiating the facts surrounding your birth? Was there a physician present? Were your parents listed? Now ask yourself, what evidence of these facts do you have for each individual on your chart?

INTERVIEWS

The traditional African *griot*, or storyteller, was a respected elder in African society. He or she was the repository of centuries-old tribal history and family lineages. Many of our contemporary elders are living griots waiting for their memories to be tapped. Elders are the genealogist's most valuable resource. Your elders may be just a visit, phone call, or letter away. Your family's elders should be your first course of research, and your first subjects. Their stories are ripe for genealogical nuggets.

Take advantage of family gatherings to interview older family

PEDIGREE CHART

DATE _____

NAME OF PERSON SUBMITTING CHART _____

STREET ADDRESS _____

CITY _____ STATE _____ ZIP _____

NO. 1 ON THIS CHART
IS THE SAME PERSON
AS NO. _____
ON CHART NO. _____

1
BORN:
WHERE:
WHEN MARRIED:
DIED:
WHERE:

NAME OF HUSBAND OR WIFE _____

SOURCE INFORMATION: _____

2
BORN:
WHERE:
WHEN MARRIED:
DIED:
WHERE:

3
BORN:
WHERE:
DIED:
WHERE:

4
BORN:
WHERE:
WHEN MARRIED:
DIED:
WHERE:

5
BORN:
WHERE:
DIED:
WHERE:

6
BORN:
WHERE:
WHEN MARRIED:
DIED:
WHERE:

7
BORN:
WHERE:
DIED:
WHERE:

8
BORN:
WHERE:
WHEN MARRIED:
DIED:
WHERE:

9
BORN:
WHERE:
DIED:
WHERE:

10
BORN:
WHERE:
WHEN MARRIED:
DIED:
WHERE:

11
BORN:
WHERE:
DIED:
WHERE:

12
BORN:
WHERE:
WHEN MARRIED:
DIED:
WHERE:

13
BORN:
WHERE:
DIED:
WHERE:

14
BORN:
WHERE:
WHEN MARRIED:
DIED:
WHERE:

15
BORN:
WHERE:
DIED:
WHERE:

16 CONTINUED ON CHART:

17 CONTINUED ON CHART:

18 CONTINUED ON CHART:

19 CONTINUED ON CHART:

20 CONTINUED ON CHART:

21 CONTINUED ON CHART:

22 CONTINUED ON CHART:

23 CONTINUED ON CHART:

24 CONTINUED ON CHART:

25 CONTINUED ON CHART:

26 CONTINUED ON CHART:

27 CONTINUED ON CHART:

28 CONTINUED ON CHART:

29 CONTINUED ON CHART:

30 CONTINUED ON CHART:

31 CONTINUED ON CHART:

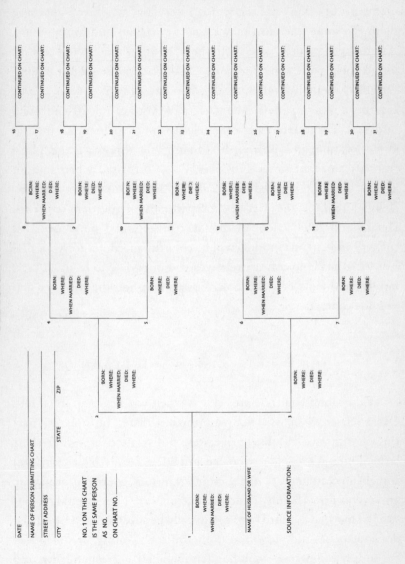

members, but don't use the word "interview" when you approach them. To some, the term may sound too serious and intimidating. Ask to "spend a little time" with them, or ask if they would be willing to "help with some questions." Make sure your subject is comfortable—mentally and physically. You have much more to gain by creating a pleasant environment, so make your contact friendly and informal. Try to interview your relatives in their home or in a favored location, and use your best manners and poise. Bring a tape recorder and take notes. However, I was surprised when an aunt agreed to be interviewed but refused to let me tape record the exchange! To direct the interview, prepare a list of questions or events. Details and recollections of the "day Jessie and I purchased that rocker" and "mama's radio" will be colorful anecdotes for your oral history. If possible, ask the relatives you interview to bring in their family heirlooms or scrapbook. Visuals help jog the memory and provide context.

The Elder—Listen and Learn

Take along your pedigree charts when you begin an interview. Older relatives can assist you with the birthdates, birthplaces, marriages, witnesses, deaths, burial sites, and relationships your chart lacks. Often it's an elder who can provide a family bible, a helpful copy of an obituary, a family's residency history, county information, and even a list of family friends and neighbors. These would be considered hard facts. Hard facts can usually be substantiated by official documents or vital records at the municipal, county, or state level. Secondary resources—including family bibles, correspondence, and diaries—can be used to confirm and establish information. Names, places, and events are often recorded in these less than authoritative sources, but they are just as reliable. The family bible is a respected and revered document in genealogical research. In many instances it is rated as a primary (hence an authoritative) resource.

Interviews would be considered tertiary resources—reliable but requiring corroboration and proof. Yes, we want the stories and all the colorful anecdotes, but you need to establish hard facts before you can get a good hold on a relative. You can often find out a lot about an older relative's parents—and their elders. What were their stories and concerns? What did they do? Where did they go? What remnants of them remain in our lives? Don't be afraid to repeat and rephrase your questions. Sometimes returning to a topic—especially with older relatives—will get better answers. If it is possible, try to revisit and share the results of your research. Always follow up with a call and a note of thanks.

Following are suggestions of subjects and questions to introduce during your interview. Keep in mind that if your goal is to find pointers to the place where your first African ancestor arrived in America, it is unlikely that these initial interviews will reveal this information outright. However, if you are patient and listen carefully you may get some valuable clues. Remember, you are now in the role of detective; much of the information you seek will not be obvious, but will have to be deciphered. Trace the path as far back as you can, taking special care to note changes in names and addresses. These could signal the steps that you seek.

Before your interview, ask your subject to gather whatever personal archives they have for you to review—letters, stories, awards, church bulletins, bibles, medals, obituaries, photographs, etc. Especially ask about the contents of the attic, garage, or an old trunk. Suggest to your relative to prepare their description of the family first: coming of age stories, funny anecdotes, recipes, and mishaps. Since family histories tend to be laced with both undesirable and possibly embarrassing events as well as high points, it is probably a good idea at the outset of the interview to remind the subject(s) that your intent is to reconstruct the past, not to hurt or judge anyone.

Reassure your subject that many past events serve to "spice up" the family history, and, in fact, the family history would be sorely lacking without these events.

Organize the interview and the data you're collecting into categories, and ask questions that fall into those categories. Memories may be triggered by the category itself. Help your subject recall the details of a scene. You want to get facts, but you also want to record vivid and lively memories. Following are possible categories and questions.

Early Life—General

Ask your relative to recall his or her earliest childhood memories:

Where and when were you born? What county and state?
How many siblings did you have?
What were your favorite toys/games?
Where did you take family excursions?
Did you go to school or work? For how long?
What was it like going to school?
What was the school building like?
Where was the school located? What county?
Do you remember the name of the teacher?
How did you get to school?
What did you eat for lunch?
When did you leave school?
Where was the house you grew up in?
How long did the family live there?
When did the family move?
Where did you go to church? What denomination?
Were you baptized/christened?
Was there a church/family cemetery?
Are family members buried there?

What were your parents like?

What did they do for a living?

Who in the family owned their own house, real estate, farm, business?

What kinds of jobs did relatives have?

Were there any other family members or boarders living with you?

Did you ever make visits to other family members? Who?

Did you own a car? What kind?

How did you celebrate the holidays?

Who were your friends/neighbors?

Were all your friends Black/Negro/colored?

Did you have any interracial relationships/friendships?

What type of meals did you have growing up?

Was there something unique your family made to eat?

Did you live on a farm or in town?

Did you have any special craft, talent, or hobby?

Who were your heroes?

Tragedies / Pitfalls

When did your (mother, father, sisters, brothers) pass/die?

How were they buried?

Where are they buried?

Were there any special burial customs?

Were there fires, storms, floods, earthquakes, or natural disasters threatening the family?

What diseases struck the family (mental and physical)?

Did you ever work outside the home?

Did you ever lose a home/job?

Were there any accidents or long-term hospitalizations in the family? How was it paid for?

Did you and other family members have insurance?

Have you ever been to court?

Celebrations

What happened when a child was born?

How did you celebrate birthdays?

What were weddings like?

Who performed the wedding?

Were there any graduations from high school, college, university, nursing school, or other trade school?

Family Culture

Would you describe your/our family as rich, poor, something in between? Why?

What kinds of jobs did your parents/siblings/spouse have? Where? What did you do for fun?

What was the family's idea of a good time?

Where did you go as a family?

What civic work was the family involved in—school, church, community, etc.?

What were the "rules of the house" for courting?

What types of clothes did you wear?

What was your favorite outfit?

Were you creative? Did you play an instrument or participate in any arts and crafts?

Did you play any sports?

What did you read?

Do you own a bible? Are there family records in the bible?

Where is the oldest family bible?

Who were your friends? What were their names? Who did the family do business with?

Education/Military/Official

Who attended college?

How was education paid for?

Were any family members in law enforcement?

Was anyone arrested/convicted/lynched? What happened?

Who in the family served in the military? Where? When? What branch? Who was discharged from the military?

Who attended trade schools? What trade?

What were the family's political affiliations?

What organizations did the family participate in? Masons? NAACP?

Historical Data

Have you ever had any encounters with famous people? What happened?

Who is the first president of the United States you remember?

What were you doing when Kennedy was assassinated?

Did you attend the 1963 March on Washington?

Where were you when you learned Dr. Martin Luther King, Jr. was assassinated? What was your/the family reaction?

How did the family survive the Depression years? Who worked? Where? What were the war years like?

How has your outlook on life changed?

How have employment and job opportunities changed?

Do you think integration worked?

What do you know about our family during slavery?

Do you know the names of family members who were slaves?

Has the family ever been attacked by racists—such as the KKK?

Are there family members who "passed" for White? Who? When? Why?

What property did the family own?

What achievement/accomplishment/writing/discovery/invention are you most proud of in the family?

Getting the most out of each interview means making sure your subject is comfortable and honest with his or her answers. Again, some questions are worth repeating because information may be later in coming to mind. Keep the interview brief—thirty or forty-five minutes—and don't press or force an issue. If you need more time or your relative is tiring, schedule another session at your subject's convenience. However, if you encounter a relative who wants to talk for hours without hesitation, be flexible and be prepared. Pack extra tapes and batteries for your tape recorder or video recorder. Always record your subject's relationship to siblings and the extended family. Interviews are a tertiary source of material, everything you hear will have to be substantiated with documentary material.

A newspaper profile of two centenarian sisters, Bessie and Sadie Delaney, became a bestselling book and play, *Having Our Say*. Their story is a great model for retelling family stories. These self-described "maiden ladies" talk about their lives and share family photographs, albums, accomplishments, and even recipes. Their story covers over 100 years of African-American history, going back to their grandmother and their parents' courtship. The locale for the article, the book, and the play is the same—the Delaney sisters' living room and kitchen!

THINGS TO LOOK FOR

Interviews help you assemble elements of texture and color in the family history—re-weaving the fabric of your past. Your next challenge is to provide documentary support for your oral histories.

Access to birth certificates, death certificates, deeds, insurance policies, wills, and the like would be a real advantage at this stage. Many of these documents can be located in public records. However, do not hesitate to ask your subjects if such documentation is in their possession. Ask to review them and make copies for your files. However, if there is resistance to letting go of material, check to see if duplicates can be obtained at the municipal building or the county clerk's office. When you borrow material, always return it promptly. You may have to pass that way again.

Organizing Data

Even at this early stage, organizing your research is extremely important. There are many systems for organizing and many kinds of organizing tools. Some genealogists keep loose-leaf notebooks, some prefer file folders, others use a computerized database. No matter what system you use, if you are very organized and maintain your records neatly, consistently, and efficiently, you won't get in your own way as you progress.

A particularly popular system among genealogists is to divide their research into surnames and geographic groups. For example, JONES-ATLANTA; JONES-NEW JERSEY; MARLEY-ATLANTA; MARLEY-VIRGINIA may be written on a tab or heading. These geographic groupings serve as dividers and contain individual entries. Entire families or family branches often moved in large numbers to the same geographic location. Knowing where various branches of the family resided will help to keep your research focused. This is especially important if your goal is to obtain the point at which your first ancestor arrived in the country. Geographically, states and counties are extremely valuable for retrieving records and historic research on your family.

Be sure to include them in your journals. An individual entry under the division MARLEY-VIRGINIA may read:

MARLEY-VIRGINIA

Telephone interview with Edna Marley Robeson in Asheboro, North Carolina on 2/12/95.

"Papa" worked as free mason in Ramseur. "Mama" was a housewife. Ten children born in Randolph County:

Edna, Mae, Dora, Fred, Lucille, Dorothy, Eugenia, Pauline, Clara, and Shelly.

Another entry may read:

MARLEY-VIRGINIA

Copied from family bible of Dora Marley Atlas, Asheboro, North Carolina on 12/26/94:

Births: Edna 2/12/12; Dora 2/2/14; Fred 5/8/16; Clara 10/6/17

Document the source from which you got the information. Keep a separate notebook for recording your interviews, noting dates and times, and the people and places you visited. Maintain an archive for your documents—it may begin as a loose-leaf notebook, move to a shoebox, and then graduate to a file cabinet. A sample Family Group Sheet is provided for you to reproduce on page 42.

As you assemble the pieces of your puzzle, you will find that new surnames enter the genealogy picture as each generation of wife, mother, and grandmother is recorded. Keeping a record of female family members requires special vigilance as women marry and assume their husband's surname. Second marriages and the children of such unions require a second pedigree and family group chart.

We Don't Talk About That

At some point in collecting research and interviews you are going to hit upon a family secret or two. Many kinds of surprises are likely to surface: incarcerations, swindles, miscegenations, "passing," adoptions, out-of-wedlock births, mental illness, and dishonorable military discharges are secrets to be found in every family history. Revealing and recording these secrets may make interviewees uncomfortable. As you become more adept at interviewing, you will learn to sidestep these issues without alienating your subject or being judgmental. Until then, move away from topics that make the interviewee uncomfortable. There will be other sources and opportunities to dig deeper.

There will also be opportunities to discern your family's participation in important movements and causes in history—especially African-American history. Was Marcus Garvey's movement important to the family? Were family members involved in the Civil Rights movement? Expect and embrace all of your ancestral surprises, secrets, and triumphs.

Purpose / Goals / Strategy

It's important to work with a goal in mind for your research. It could be to write a family history book, to organize a family reunion, to follow the six generations on your father's side, or to find your African ancestor. A goal gives your research focus and purpose and moves your project forward. It's very easy to get involved in pursuing information that delays and distracts you from your goal. Your goal can be very large or very small. And it can change along the way. I began by looking for a Taylor family reunion and ended up writing a book. Starting a family reunion is a popular and very achievable goal. Locating and reuniting family for perhaps the first

FAMILY GROUP RECORD

HUSBAND _____

OCCUPATIONS: _____

BORN: _____ PLACE: _____

CHRISTENED: _____ PLACE: _____

MARRIED: _____ PLACE: _____

DIED: _____ PLACE: _____

BURIED: _____ PLACE: _____

HUSBAND'S FATHER _____ HUSBAND'S MOTHER _____

HUSBAND'S OTHER WIVES _____

WIFE _____

OCCUPATIONS: _____

BORN: _____ PLACE: _____

CHRISTENED: _____ PLACE: _____

DIED: _____ PLACE: _____

BURIED: _____ PLACE: _____

WIFE'S FATHER _____ WIFE'S MOTHER _____

WIFE'S OTHER HUSBANDS _____

CHILDREN

SEX M/F	GIVEN NAMES SURNAME	WHEN BORN DAY MONTH YEAR			WHERE BORN TOWN	COUNTY	STATE/COUNTY	DATE OF FIRST MARRIAGE	FIRST SPOUSE	WHEN DIED D/M/Y
1										
2										
3										
4										
5										
6										
7										
8										
9										
10										

OTHER MARRIAGES:

SOURCE INFORMATION:

time—at the family homestead or on a bittersweet odyssey to a slave plantation—can be the culmination of a family history project.

Books on family history can be an ongoing project for the whole family. Self-published books of family history are valuable compilations of family lore. You never know until you start looking and asking if anyone has written a book about a branch of your family. Such reconstructions can be brimming with anecdotes and minutiae. These small books usually run the gamut of credibility and detail. Sometimes they're less involved with establishing hard facts and more concerned with lore, legend, and story. They are usually published in connection with a family reunion project, and copies are distributed to local historical societies, libraries, and genealogical societies.

Creating an extensive family chart that goes back for generations is sometimes a goal in and of itself. The image of a huge tree with sprawling branches covered with leaves, and a name on each leaf, is the picture most people envision when they think about family history projects. Some genealogical hobbyists are less interested in the "life and times" aspect of an ancestor and simply want to chart, expand, and establish a breadth of reach and ancestral connection.

Whatever your goal, whether to track a prune pudding recipe or find your African ancestor who first arrived on a slave ship, you are assembling a puzzle. Piece by piece, the whole picture will emerge. Expect your progress to be slow but steady. Each clue, like signs on a highway, will show the way to the next clue. By following this trail of clues, we can arrive at our final destination. There is no substitute for perseverance and determination.

4

WHAT AM I LOOKING FOR?

LISTENING

If you listen carefully to what your interviewees have to say, you'll be able to look for the sources to corroborate their stories. Hopefully the interviews you have completed with elders have revealed new names of people and places to add to your research picture. Perhaps you've even acquired names of their elders and approximations of their ages. During the interviews, one of the things you want most to do is connect your family history to people (family friends, elders, neighbors), places (births, marriages, deaths), and even things (deeds, bibles, address books). Try to establish the migratory pattern of your relatives. Did they move from the south to the northern part of the country? From the south to the midwest? Listen for the names of towns, states, cities, and addresses. But pay special attention to the names of counties. The county seat will most often be the repository of the documents you need—those vital documents.

Information from your interview will also help you anchor certain events in time. Stories of land deals, changes, and exchanges may be juxtaposed against Aunt Gwen's story about Papa selling the farm. Recounts of specific events will help you with dates and time periods when you're looking for records of deeds, wills, birth certificates, and the like. Knowing what kinds of cars, music, and clothing were prevalent during certain events may help you differentiate a story in the 1920s from one in the 1930s.

LOOKING

The more you know about history—especially the history of the state you are researching—the better. Read a book or two about Blacks in the World Wars, the Depression, Reconstruction, or wherever you are in your pedigree chart. If you want to research family members in various branches of the military and you are not knowledgeable about this subject, check out the young adult section of the public library. These books are often quite sufficient to get you over small hurdles. They don't even have to be African-American history books because what you'll need is a feel for the time and place in which your relative lived. Having this historic perspective will help you supplement, explain, and magnify your relative's story.

After you have acquired a list of names, dates, and places from your interview, you can start finding names in public records. Since 1790, the U.S. federal government has administered a census of the country's population every ten years. With each decade, the census collected more and more detail about the population. Census records are the pivotal pieces of information for the genealogist. At different census polls, this demographic data was augmented, modified, and categorized in new ways. After it was organized this data was made available to social and behavioral scientists and their agencies. These scientists analyzed census counts and issued reports—vital statistics—about national, state, and county populations. Vital statistics are records of the births, deaths, marriages, health, and disease within a principality—city, county, town, state, etc. Since 1914, it has been federal law that states maintain repositories of this information. Records compiled before 1914 vary in completeness and usefulness, yet these records are an essential tool of the genealogist.

Access to vital records vary from government to government, state to state, municipality to municipality. Birth certificates, death certificates, social security payments, pensions, and welfare may all be available but access requirements may vary widely within a jurisdiction. A state-by-state sampling of available materials is included in the local resources section of this book.

Using census data, government officials could spot trends in national migration and population and make policy and planning projections accordingly. In the process of making these aggregate head counts, information had to be gathered on individuals, their family members, and neighboring environs. Because some of the data contained information about individual families and their residency circumstances, these records proved useful to the family historian. It is important to keep in mind that the census was not created as a genealogist's tool.

In most large libraries, the latest census is a part of the collection. It exists as a series of encyclopedic charts and tables in either bound or electronic format usually organized by state. This is aggregate census information—a profile of the entire population based on analyses of individual household information by the aforementioned experts. This is not what you need. Remember the census is an attempt to account for *each individual* residing in *each household* of the United States since 1790. Therefore, miles of individual microfilm and microfiche exist. These individual household census records are accessible only in major genealogical collections. The National Archives, the Library of Congress, and the Family History Centers of the Family History Library in Salt Lake City, are the most commonly used repositories of these records. It is these individual census records that you need for your family research. Copies made from these very old records can be messy and hard to read. Blank sample forms are in chapter 13 for you to reproduce and transfer information onto.

Before attempting to use census data, it is useful to know a few facts about the census itself. Its colorful and volatile evolution is particularly important to the African-American genealogist.

The United States Decennial Census is the most frequently used genealogical resource. It often provides the most essential fact we're looking for—a name. You may be fortunate enough to get the birthdate and address as well. It is the most comprehensive historic listing of individual persons in the United States and for that reason it is an essential tool even though it is often flawed. Bias and illiteracy can be seen on both sides of a census document. Sometimes the household members may have given erroneous or misleading information. Also, census takers' handwriting was not always clear and legible. They sometimes didn't understand the names of the people they were counting—especially unique and exotic sounding names of the African diaspora. The further back into the 19th and 18th century you take your research, the more obstacles you will find. You may be looking for people who were regarded by the government as nameless and not worth counting.

But that isn't always the case. *Free Black Heads of Families in the First Census of the United States* is a separate report on the Black population within the 1790 census. However, the report is limited because it lists only the number of Black and mixed blood persons living in the home without supplying their names; only the head of the household is named. Such a census could be useful for establishing a household by identifying neighbors. In 1820, free Blacks were listed by age groups. The report titled *Free Negro Heads of Families in the United States in 1830* was compiled by Carter G. Woodson and serves as an index to the Black persons represented in that census. It is also a source that identifies Black slaveowners, which was sometimes the condition under which families "bought their freedom" and that of family members before Emancipation. The 1850 census was the first to list the entire household of free Blacks by name, age, sex, race, occupation, and birthplace.

Slave schedules were included within each census, but they were only head counts. In 1850 and 1860, slave schedules included the age and sex of slaves tied to an owner. By 1870, all persons—Black and White—were listed by name. From 1870 to 1920, the genealogy methodology is the same for all races. However, it is frustrating when there are errors, omissions, misplaced and destroyed records, and illegible handwriting to contend with.

Be careful not to eliminate a European ancestor or an ancestor who may be listed as White by relying solely on Black genealogy sources. In the 1830 census, at least two free Blacks' wives were listed as White.

FEDERAL CENSUS CATEGORIES, 1790–1920

CENSUS OF 1790:

Name of head of family
address
number of free white males of 16 years and up, including heads
free white males under 16
free white females, including heads
all other free persons
number of slaves

CENSUS OF 1800:

Name of head of family
address
number of free white males under 10 years of age
number of free white males aged 10 and under 16

number of free white males aged 16 and under 26

number of free white males aged 26 and under 45

number of free white males aged 45 and upwards

all other free persons, except Indians not taxed

number of slaves

CENSUS OF 1810:

Name of head of family

address

number of free white males and females under 10 years of age

number of free white males and females aged 10 and under 16

number of free white males and females aged 16 and under 26

number of free white males and females aged 26 and under 45

number of free white males and females aged 45 and upward

all other free persons, except Indians not taxed

number of slaves

CENSUS OF 1820:

Name of head of family

address

number of free white males and females under 10 years of age

number of free white males and females aged 10 and under 16

number of free white males and females aged 16 and under 26

number of free white males and females aged 26 and under 45

number of free white males and females aged 45 and upwards

number of free white males between 16 and 18 years

foreigners not naturalized

males and female slaves and free colored persons under 14 years

males and female slaves and free colored persons aged 14 and under 26

males and female slaves and free colored persons aged 26 and under 45 males and female slaves and free colored persons aged 45 and upwards

all other free persons, except Indians not taxed

number of persons (including slaves) engaged in agriculture, commerce and manufacture

CENSUS OF 1830:

Name of head of family

address

number of free white males and females in 5-year groups to 20

number of free white males and females in 10-year groups from 20-100

number of free white males and females aged 100 and over

number of slaves and free colored persons in six broad age groups

number of deaf and dumb under 14

number of deaf and dumb aged 14 to 24

number of deaf and dumb aged 25 and upwards

number of blind

foreigners not naturalized

CENSUS OF 1840:

Name of head of family

address

number of free white males and females in 5-year age group to 20

number of free white males and females in 10-year age groups from 20 to 100

number of free white males and females aged 100 and upwards

number of slaves and free colored persons in six broad age groups

number of deaf and dumb

number of blind

number of insane and idiotic in public and private charge

number of persons in each family employed in each of seven classes of occupations

number of schools and number of scholars

number of white persons over 20 who could not read and write

number of pensioners for Revolutionary or military service

CENSUS OF 1850:

Name

address

age

sex

color (white, black, or mulatto) for each person

whether deaf and dumb, blind, insane or idiotic

all free persons required to give value of real estate owned

profession, occupation or trade for each male person over 15

place of birth

whether married within the year

whether attended school within the year

whether unable to read and write for persons over 20

whether a pauper or a convict

CENSUS OF 1860:

Name

Address

Age

Sex

Color (white, black, mulatto) for each person

Whether deaf and dumb, blind, insane or idiotic

All free persons required to give value of real estate and of personal estate owned

Profession, occupation or trade for each male and female over 15

Place of birth (State, Territory, or Country)
Whether married within the year
Whether attended school within the year
Whether unable to read and write for persons over 20
Whether pauper or convict

CENSUS OF 1870:
Address
Name
Age
Sex
Color (including Chinese and Indian)
Citizenship for males over 21
Profession, occupation or trade
Value of real estate
Value of personal estate
Place of birth
Whether father and mother were foreign born
Born within the year
Married within the year
Attended school within the year
For person 10 years old and over, whether able to read and write
Whether deaf and dumb, blind, insane or idiotic

CENSUS OF 1880:
Address
Name
Relation to head of Family
Sex
Race
Age
Marital Status
Born within the year

Married within the year

Profession, occupation or trade

Number of months unemployed during census year

Whether person is sick or temporarily disabled so as to be unable to attend to ordinary business or duties

If so, what is the sickness or disability

Whether blind, deaf and dumb, idiotic, insane, maimed, crippled or bedridden

Attended school within the year

Ability to read and write

Place of birth of person, father and mother

CENSUS OF 1890

More than 99 percent of this census was destroyed by fire in 1921

CENSUS OF 1900

Address

Name

Relationship to family head

Sex

Race

Age

Marital Status

Number of years married

For women, number of children born and number now living

Birthplace of person and parents

If foreign born, year of immigration and whether naturalized

Occupation

Months not employed

School attendance

Literacy

Ability to speak English

Whether on a farm

Home owned or rented, and if owned, whether mortgaged

(supplemental schedules for the blind and deaf)

Census of 1910

Address

Name

Relationship to family head

Sex

Race

Age

Marital Status

Number of year of present marriage

For women, number of children born and number now living

Birthplace and mother tongue of persons and parent

If foreign born, year of immigration

Whether naturalized and whether able to speak English, or if
   not, language spoken

Occupation, industry and class of worker

If an employee, whether out of work during year

Literacy

School attendance

Home owned or rented

Whether farm or house

Whether a survivor of Union or Confederate Army or Navy

Whether blind or deaf and dumb

Census of 1920

Address

Name

Relationship to family head

Sex

Race

Age

Marital status

If foreign born, year of immigration to the U.S., whether naturalized, and year of naturalization

School attendance

Literacy

Birthplace of person and parents

Mother tongue of foreign born

Ability to speak English

Occupation, industry and class or worker

Home owned or rented

If owned, whether mortgaged

For non-farm mortgaged, market value, original amount of mortgage, balance due, interest rate

Remember: To protect individual privacy, individual records are only available 72 years before the current year, so the 1920 census is the most recent census schedule for individuals available. The 1930 census will be available in 2002.

5

WHAT'S IN A NAME?

PEOPLE, PLACES, THINGS

It starts with you. Your birth name marks the beginning of your search. Your given name and any records associated with your name are the center of your research. Your birth records—societal and medical—linked your parents. Your parents' records—marriage certificates, wills, deeds, contracts, and birth certificates—will link you to past generations. Who are you beyond your name? What anecdotal information would point to relations and relationships? Do you keep a journal? Have you written or recorded a mini-autobiography? These are the kinds of objects and records you are seeking among your family.

There are various tools you can use when trying to "flesh out" a name. Names collected from the oral tradition can be used to determine and locate family. Useful clues can be discerned in the history behind "family names," "nicknames," "aliases," and "name changes." Consider them when doing your research because names are a real nuisance for the genealogist—Black or White. When tracing a name—even back one generation—variant spellings and pronunciations can cause a researcher to spend hours searching the wrong records. It can be enormously frustrating to discover that you have spent hours trying to locate "John" only to find out that "John John" was really the nickname for "James" or "Jacob."

In 1877, after Emancipation, Augusta, GA, listed these as the fifteen most common surnames of former slaves: Williams, Thomas, Robinson, Jones, Brown, Scott, Johnson, Walker, Harris, Smith, Davis, Turner, Jackson, Green, and Anderson. Slaves often chose surnames for themselves—"titles"—that were independent of and unknown by the slavemaster. This makes it even more difficult to connect the name of a free person of color to records from his or her life in slavery. But even in the 18th and 19th century, African-American families strove to maintain a connection to family. You may find early ancestors if the names of the first African ancestors were kept in memory and family tradition.

African-American soldiers during the American Revolution chose surnames when they were given the opportunity—either keeping the name of their former slavemaster or selecting one of their own. Freeman (the most popular), Rogers, Liberty, Ball, Phillips, Johnson, Caesar, Rhodes, Brown, Jackson, Vassal, and Green were among the African-American surnames of the soldiers included in the Fourth Connecticut Regiment or the American Revolution.

There can also be dozens of spellings and pronunciations of the same name within a family for a variety of deliberate or inadvertent reasons: families separated and migrated to different areas; literacy rates varied widely; census takers and county recorders made mistakes; and people wanted to conceal their identity. Errors and omissions in family names and personal names should be expected, which is why you need to locate corroborating information. Records written by hand are a challenge for the genealogist. Handwritten census records—especially when viewed on microfilm—are not always legible. The deciphering of penmanship and placing it into historical context is a professional specialty.

There were as many as thirteen spellings of Faulkner in 1790. Consider variant spellings with any family name you are researching. You should imagine, collect, and record as many variants in the spelling of surnames as possible. Such an exercise makes it easier when scrolling through yards of microfilm to spot an inconsistency in spelling that might be another branch of the same family.

Williamson	Wilemson	Wilson
Jamison	Jamieson	Jameson
Perrault	Perot	Poirot

Would you believe the English surname "Enroughty" is sometimes pronounced "Darby?" Well, it's the kind of thing that makes genealogy a special challenge. Nicknames and pet names are another genealogy headache. You'll find the inevitable, "Oh, there's a John Senior and John John. But we always called the younger John Clarence!" What can you do when the only name you've found for a relative is a nickname? The cycle of interviewing relatives and seeking documentation begins. Pronunciation and spelling vary with all names—seek additional proof in vital records. Look for authenticated business records, interview friends and associates, look through personal records, and persevere!

Government records can be culled for military, humanitarian, social, legal, and professional research on a name. Federal, state, municipal, and county jurisdictions all have some archival and historical resources on a variety of activities and concerns. They may not provide information about a specific individual, but they may provide useful historical information and context.

Even driving records can be a useful source of genealogical information. Such records are stored at the department of motor vehicles, county clerks office, or municipal clerk's office and can be inspected in person. Or you can initiate a search in writing for a small fee, usually under $20 dollars per name. Directories of fraternal, social, and benevolent societies can be useful in tracking names of beneficiaries and benefactors of charitable crusades and movements. And business records, such as banking records, contracts, loans, liens, and leases, usually contain information and circumstances related to names.

PLACES

Matching names and places is fundamental to a genealogy project. To legitimize your research, you must have vital records. Also, deeds, property records, tombstones, cemeteries and burial record documents are available from various levels of government. Unsubstantiated facts should not be incorporated into a serious genealogy project. But keep the stories in mind; proof may come to you further down the road.

TIME

Recording dates can be done in a variety of styles: Month/Day/Year is what is commonly used in the United States while Day/Month/Year is common in Europe. Also the Gregorian calendar we use was created in the 16th century, but many countries continued to use the older Julian calendar. If you pursue your roots into the 18th century, you may have to compensate for these co-existing calendars. It is a common problem addressed in books, on websites and within genealogical support groups.

SOUNDS

The smart people at the Census Bureau developed a tool to help people researching names. Since 1880, the census has been indexed by a unique index called Soundex. It is a code designed to link names that may sound or be spelled alike in the same file. The index begins with the 1880 census. If you do not know where an ancestor lived, this tool will help you search the census more quickly. The first letter of the surname is the first element in the code. Calculate the remaining three-digit code using the Soundex formula. Strike out the vowels a, e, i, o, u and y, w, and h. Find the corresponding numbers for the remaining letters using the following key:

1	BPFV
2	CSKGJQXZ

3	DT
4	L
5	M N
6	R

Code names that have prefixes (Le, De, Van, etc.) with and without the prefix and look for the name on both rolls of microfilm. Mc and Mac are not considered prefixes in Soundex. Double letters should be treated as one letter (for example, the second "L" in Lloyd is striked out). Names with letters side by side that have the same number on the Soundex should be treated as one letter. If a two letter code is the result, add zero to the end. For example, SMITH = S M(5) I(X) T(3) H(X), the I and H are DISREGARDED and zero added to yield a three-digit code, S 530; BROWN = B R(6) O(X) W(X) N(5), the O and W are DISREGARDED and a zero added for code, B 650.

The code is your indicator and guide to the census microfilm and should be used on variant spellings of the same surname. You will research one name (code) at a time. After you have determined your Soundex code, go to the microfilm guides, which are arranged by state, then first letter of the surname, and then chronologically by Soundex code. Soundex is available for 1880, 1900, and 1920 census schedules. The National Archives publishes booklets on the availability and film numbers of specific cities and booklets will be available. Having a working knowledge of Soundex will make your research move along more smoothly.

There are survivals of African language throughout the Black experience. From Haitian "voodoo" to Trinidadian "calypso" and Jamaican "rastafari," the roots of Africa burst forth. Yoruba, Ibo, Hausa, and Wolof are among the African languages that were common in slave trading principalities and still are spoken. These unique sounds and language patterns may survive in your family history. Listen for words about family, slavery, places, children, descendants, water, and boats. These terms are common in familiar storytelling throughout the African diaspora.

Things to Look For

Probably the one thing that brings most information to genealogy is the family Bible. The front pages of the bible are often used to list the names and bithdates of children in succession, and such bibles are sought out and indexed by genealogical societies, especially the Family History Library in Salt Lake City.

There are other ways that names can help you trace your ancestry to Africa. Names of ships, ports, or auctions can provide clues to your heritage. Bills of sales, emancipation papers, cargo lists, diaries, journals, and plantation records may contain valuable clues to some "thing" that can connect your ancestral bloodlines. A drum figured prominently in Alex Haley's quest for "The African." Haley knew his progenitor was a young west African teen who was kidnapped and sold into slavery while out searching for materials to make a drum. While Haley's Tennessee memories of stories, names, and places pointed to Gambia, it was story of the drum making that connected Haley to Kunta Kinte and Tennessee to Juffre.

There are powerful ancestral messages in some of the things our families hold on to. Inquire about the furniture in your ancestral home—there may be a story there. Quilts, jewelry, silverware, and various knick-knacks may have value to your research as stories are passed along with an heirloom.

6

LOCAL SOURCES

THE PUBLIC LIBRARY

Your local public library is rich with genealogy resources and people-finding tools. Municipal libraries are not only repositories of books and periodicals, many now offer access to the Internet, commercial databases, and online services. They are worth visiting with your questions clearly outlined and your charts and files in hand. Some of your questions about names, dates, and events can be answered and a plan can be designed for more in-depth research. Inquire about genealogy workshops sponsored by the library. Biographies, autobiographies, geographic encyclopedias, local histories, address directories, and subject indexes can provide facts and details to help fill gaps within your family history.

The library is also where you can get a speedy education or refresher on Black and African-American history. African-American history is undergoing a lively renaissance and revision. New books of historical merit and genealogical credibility are published regularly.

Local libraries often specialize in the history of its municipality. If you are researching the community you're living in, the neighborhood library is the first place you want to check. Here you can find out when, where, and how the African presence in your municipality was first recorded. Where were the earliest Black communities established? What were the names of those cities and towns? Who were the founders? Were the founders slave or free—refugee slaves, emancipated, or freeman? What industry dominated the region? Are there records on the transfer of goods and services among landholders and sharecroppers? Are there slave or freeman narratives in the library? Are there local scholars who have studied the Black demography and migration in the region? Are they available for an interview?

If you are looking for a specific fact, you can find an enormous amount of information in the library serving your ancestor's community. For example, "When was Randolph County created? What was that area called before? Is there a map of the earlier county? Where are the county records?" These questions can be answered at the county, state, or genealogical library.

The Librarian

Initiate your research at the reference librarian's desk. He or she can refer you to the most appropriate resources. Librarians will not do your research for you, but they will help with strategy and approach. You should have specific questions in mind before you involve the librarian in your project. Over time, you may find your librarian acquiring a special interest in you and your subject. Cultivating a relationship with the reference librarian can expedite your research. Almost every day new information becomes available to the public, and the librarian is often the gatekeeper of that information.

The Library Collection

Following is a brief refresher on useful items you can find in the library to move your research forward.

The Catalog

You may be lucky enough to find a family history in the local library. Scores of hours of research may be shaved off your genealogical efforts if you find a book about a branch of the family you are researching that has already been published. Look up the family name in the library catalog and you may find that a cousin has already begun compiling a genealogy.

The catalog is your guide to the contents of the library. The librarian can assist you, because these days the catalog may be in book, microfilm, or electronic form rather than the traditional card catalog so many of us remember. Still, the principle remains the same. Information is grouped by title, subject, or author. Personal name, keyword, organization, association, and publication year may be other searchable features in the catalog. Remember "title" can be the title of a book, folder, photograph, or almost any other item in the library's collection. The same item will usually be cross-referenced by subject. As a search term, "author" is self-explanatory, but not every author is a human. Institutions, organizations, and agencies author books, periodicals, and special reports. This is especially true when looking for directories of social, fraternal, or religious organizations.

Biographies

Biographies are written accounts of individual lives. They are a natural stepping-stone for the genealogist. Because you are looking for a specific person, there may be a biography on your relative or your relative may have been related either personally or professionally to the subject of a biography. Don't forget that not every biography makes it to a bestseller list or even your local bookstore. You may find a self-published book or a modest book of memoirs you can use. If you believe your relative was involved with a prominent person of the time or in the area, look for a biography of that person. Then check the notes and index to see if your ancestor is cited. Usually, we think biographies constitute the lives of people, but they can also be written about the lives of animals, such as race horses. When trying to locate 19th century Negro jockeys for a research project, I found most of the athletes' names when searching for information about the horses!

Autobiographies

Autobiographies are books that recount the author's own life. Again, these books can be useful genealogical research. There were significant numbers of African-Americans who published their "stories." Frederick Douglas's narrative, *My Bondage and My Freedom*, is one of the most widely known examples, but there are also treatises on the lives of Black cowboys, businessmen, writers, and artists whose names are not recorded in popular history. Use the index of autobiographies to locate these names.

Atlases and Geographic Encyclopedias

Gazetteers are handy guides to geographical changes. They are essentially dictionaries that include descriptive information on cities, populations, mountains, counties, and industry. Consult them to establish the history of a place. They are extremely useful in establishing historical county data.

Directories

A directory is generally a list of people and locations. The most commonly used directories are telephone and address directories. Some libraries and historical societies save old directories on microfilm. Use them to locate people in municipalities, cities, and towns. Specific directories for organizations—fraternal, professional, and social—are also useful peoplefinding aides.

Indexes

Your local library can help you find out what is in the library collections of other cities, states, countries, organizations, and associations. Paperbound and electronic indexes are pointers to resources outside the local library. Indexes differ from catalogs in that they will not provide you with the artifact but simply tell you that a thing exists. It's like finding the title of an audio recording and then trying to find a store that carries the recording in the format you need.

Don't worry if it all sounds confusing. The advantage of electronic library records is that the library user can search the catalog by a single keyword, which can be an author, subject, or title. Keyword searching gives you more information than you want or need; however, it results in a thorough search of the catalog.

THE FAMILY HISTORY LIBRARY OF THE CHURCH OF JESUS CHRIST OF LATTER-DAY SAINTS

The Family History Library (FHL) contains the world's largest collection of genealogical data. The FHL is located in Salt Lake City, Utah, and was founded in 1884 by the Church of Jesus Christ of Latter-Day Saints (Mormons). Branches of the FHL are called Family History Centers (FHCs) and are linked to the FHL collection by a network of computers, CD-Roms, and interlibrary loans. There are over 2,000 FHCs operating in the world, making the FHL the largest and most accessible collection of birth, marriage, death, military, land, and probate documents available. The FHL has a database of genealogical records that could immediately fill the gaps in your family chart. As incredible as it is to imagine, the FHL has over 2 billion individuals in its genealogical system. There are almost 200 teams of researchers traveling around the world recording data to augment the collection. The unique mission of the members of the church is to link the "family of man" in a covenant of love and service. This covenant does not end with death but extends to the spirit world of our ancestors.

This global mission is an advantage to everyone pursuing genealogy. Teams of researchers go out from the FHL to catalog, classify, microfilm, and record information from almost any resource and location you can imagine, covering all periods of recorded history. The extent of the FHL collection runs from family bibles to social security records.

There was a time when Blacks were not welcome participants in the church's genealogical efforts, but those ideas have changed and the FHCs welcome and encourage everyone to include their genealogy in the "family" archives. Take advantage of your place in history and use the FHL centers liberally. The resources they have compiled are mind-boggling, and a visit to an FHL can almost be one-stop shopping for your project. Their interloan services and depth of research are the most accessible, economical, and exhaustive in the world. Chances are there is one near your hometown or county seat. Take advantage of the vast genealogical resources available there. Call 1-800-346-6044 to find a Family History Center in your area.

GENEALOGICAL SOCIETIES

Genealogical societies often build independent collections specializing in an area's local and regional genealogical needs. They are good resources to consult when you are trying to comprehend the specialized genealogical intricacies of handwriting, court records, and calendar changes.

HISTORICAL SOCIETIES

Historical societies are valuable resources to consult when you need to know what happened in a county, city, or state. Their files of chronologies and events for a region are usually more detailed and specialized than resources for the general public.

CHAMBERS OF COMMERCE

Consult the chamber of commerce when you are looking for business history or have industrial, commercial, and revenue related queries. Most chambers of commerce keep records indefinitely as business relationships tend to require documentation and reexamination.

STATES

Statehood in our country is a curious subject because each state has its own unique evolutionary history. The history of a region as it evolved to statehood is a social, political, and economic story. With each decade, those conditions changed and developed, defining its population. African-American history is a part of regional history, so it would be wise to become familiar with the history of the state you're researching. But you will undoubtedly read general history books too, because your family research can be enhanced by how much you know. Sometimes a Black population reacted to state-issued edicts and laws. Knowledge of a state's Black migration will help you understand how and why families moved to certain areas at certain times. Often the migration was voluntary, but sometimes terror campaigns against Blacks would force a family or entire community to move. Like the Native Americans, Blacks migrated as borders, boundaries, statehood restrictions, or freedoms loomed.

7

NATIONAL SOURCES

The United States government has resources that are useful to your ancestral search. The records were collected for purposes other than genealogy, but they do record the lives and transactions of individuals. America's institutional racism often segregates the African-American records, but they are there. African-Americans held residences, paid taxes, served in wars, built schools, patented inventions and owned property.

The National Archives and Records Administration (NARA), Seventh and Pennsylvania Avenue, NW, Washington DC 20408; (202) 501-5400, collects, organizes, preserves and makes available documents from American history. Here you will find pension records, military records, census records and more. The various government agencies that touched the life of the Black American left a paper legacy here that includes Freedmen's Bureau and military service records. Use these sources at one of NARA's regional centers. They are located in Waltham, MA, (617) 647-8100; New York City, NY, (212) 337-1300; Philadelphia, PA, (218) 597-3000; Chicago, IL, (312) 353-0162; East Point, GA, (404) 763-7477; Kansas City, MO, (816) 926-6272; Fort Worth, TX, (817) 334-5525; Denver, CO, (303) 236-0817; San Bruno, CA, (415) 876-9009; Laguna Niguel,

CA, (714) 643-4241; Seattle, WA, (206) 526-6507; and Anchorage, AK, (907) 271-2441.

At the state level you will find more specific and specialized resources. The assistance of state genealogical societies, historical societies and state libraries will lead you to vital records, cemeteries, courthouses, independent publications and bookstores.

STATE BY STATE RESOURCES

Alabama (www.state.al.us)

Alabama Genealogical Society
Samford University
PO Box 2296
Birmingham, AL 35229-0001
(205) 870-2749

Alaska (www.state.ak.us)

Alaska Genealogical Society
7030 Dickerson Drive
Anchorage, AK 99504

Genealogical Society of Southeast Alaska
518 Deermount
PO Box 6313
Ketchikan, AK 99901
Promotes and supports local efforts to collect and maintain genealogical records. Contains member's pedigrees, local records, and information concerning the society.

Arizona (www.state.az.us)

Genealogical Society of Arizona
2132 E. Gemini Drive
Tempe, AZ 85283-3320

Arizona State Genealogical Society
PO Box 42075
Tucson, AZ 85733-2075
Researches and publishes genealogical records. Sponsors classes, seminars, and research trips.

Arkansas (www.state.ar.us)

Ark-La-Tex Genealogical Association
PO Box 4462
Shreveport, LA 71134-0462
(318) 687-3673
FOUNDED: 1955. For genealogists whose interests lie in the South, especially in the states of Arkansas, Louisiana, and Texas. Collects, preserves, and makes available genealogical materials, documents, and records and encourages interest in genealogy and sponsors educational programs for its development.

Arkansas Genealogical Society
PO Box 908
Hot Springs, AR 71902
(501) 262-4513
Provides primary and secondary source materials to researchers of family history. Conducts educational programs.

Melting Pot Genealogical Society (MPGS)
PO Box 936
Hot Springs, AR 71902
(501) 262-4679

FOUNDED: 1977. Conducts genealogical research in Hot Springs, Arkansas. Operates genealogical library that is open to the public.

California (www.state.ca.us)

Los Californianos
c/o Beatric C. Turner
Box 1693
San Leandro, CA 94577-0169
(510) 276-5429
FOUNDED: 1969. Descendants of the Spanish who arrived in Alta (upper) California before February 2, 1848. Libraries, historical organizations, and schools are historical or corresponding members. Seeks to preserve the heritage of the early Spanish Californians in Alta California; provides authentic interpretation of Alta California's history via oral, written, pictorial, or other methods. Conducts research of genealogical, civil, religious, military, and cultural activities in Alta California. Sponsors historic speakers.

California Genealogical Society (CGS)
Box 77105
San Francisco, CA 94107
(415) 777-9936
FOUNDED: 1898. Promotes genealogical research. Organizes discussion groups. Sponsors workshops, seminars, and fairs. Conducts luncheons and fundraising activities. Maintains speakers' bureau.

California History Society
678 Mission Street
San Francisco, CA 94105

Colorado (www.state.co.us)

Colorado Council of Genealogical Societies
PO Box 24379
Denver, CO 80224-0379
FOUNDED: 1979. Coordinates genealogical societies throughout Colorado. Provides information to genealogical societies about education, membership, and community service.

Colorado Genealogical Society (CGS)
PO Box 9218
Denver, CO 80209-9218
(303) 571-1535
FOUNDED: 1924. Promotes genealogy in Colorado. Seeks to locate, preserve, and index historical records; assists and supports state libraries.

Colorado Preservation Alliance (CPA)
c/o Colorado State Archives
1313 Sherman Street
Denver, CO 80203
FOUNDED: 1989. Librarians, archivists, curators, records managers, and genealogists united to promote preservation of records and documents, and to coordinate archival research and education.

Connecticut (www.state.ct.us)

Connecticut Genealogical Society
PO Box 435
Glastonbury, CT 06033-0435
(203) 569-0002

Connecticut Society of Genealogists (CSG)
PO Box 435
Glastonbury, CT 06033-0435
(203) 569-0002
FOUNDED: 1968. Promotes genealogical research.

Delaware (www.state.de.us)

Anonymous Families History Project
c/o Prof. Tamara K. Hareven
University of Delaware
Department of Individual and Family Studies
101 Alison Hall
Newark, DE 19716
(302) 831-6500
FOUNDED: 1971. Steering committee of twelve is composed of faculty members at colleges and universities, mostly historians. Participating scholars encourage their students to write the social histories (as distinct from genealogies) of their own families and to deposit them in the Anonymous Family History Archive at the University of Minnesota, a component of the Social Welfare History Archives Center. Conducts research and issues packet of instructional materials.

Delaware Genealogical Society
505 N. Market Street
Wilmington, DE 19801-3091
(302) 655-7161
FOUNDED: 1977. Records repositories in Delaware and donates genealogy information to libraries.

District of Columbia (www.hswdc.org)
Historical Society of Washington, D.C.
1307 New Hampshire Avenue, N.W.
Washington, DC 20036-1507

Florida (www.state.fl.us)

Florida Genealogical Society
PO Box 18624
Tampa, FL 33629-8624
(813) 251-8694
FOUNDED: 1958. Serves individuals in Hillsborough County, Florida, interested in the study of family histories. Promotes the development and use of improved research techniques. Conducts workshops and seminars. Maintains speakers bureau.

Florida State Genealogical Society
PO Box 10249
Tallahassee, FL 32302-2249

Georgia (www.state.ga.us)

First Families of Georgia 1733–1797
15 Watson Drive
Newnan, GA 30263
FOUNDED: 1986. Individuals that are able to substantiate lineal descent from an ancestor who settled in Georgia between 1733 and 1797. Promotes interest in and study of the history, culture, and traditions of Georgia. Semiannual convention—always February and November in Georgia.

Georgia Genealogical Society (GGS)
PO Box 54575
Atlanta, GA 30308-0575
FOUNDED: 1964.

Georgia Historical Society
501 Whitaker Street
Savannah, GA 31499

Hawaii (www.state.hi.us)

Hawaii County Genealogical Society
PO Box 831
Keaau, HI 96749
(808) 965-6408

Idaho (www.state.id.us)

Idaho Genealogical Society
4620 Overland Road, No. 204
Boise, ID 83705
(208) 384-0542
FOUNDED: 1961. Compiles and preserves historical and genealogical records pertaining to Idaho. Conducts genealogical research and educational programs.

Illinois (www.state.il.us)

Illinois State Genealogical Society (ISGS)
PO Box 10195
Springfield, IL 62791
(217) 789-1968
FOUNDED: 1968. Individuals interested in genealogy. Seeks to further genealogical research.

Indiana (www.state.in.us)

Indiana Genealogical Society
PO Box 10507
Ft. Wayne, IN 46852-0507
FOUNDED: 1988. Members may be individuals or organizations. The purpose of the society is to promote genealogical and historical research and education; preserve and safeguard manuscripts, books, cemeteries, and memorabilia relating to Indiana and its people; and

assist in the publication of materials about the people, places, institutions, and organizations of Indiana.

Iowa (www.state.ia.us)

Iowa Genealogical Society
PO Box 7735
Des Moines, IA 50322-7735
(515) 276-0287

State Historical Society of Iowa
600 E. Locust
Des Moines, IA 50319

Kansas (www.state.ks.us)

American Family Records Association
PO Box 15505
Kansas City, MO 64106
(816) 252-0950
FOUNDED: 1978. Institutes and individuals including genealogists, historians, and adoptologists seeking to improve education and availability of information in the fields of family history, genealogy, local history, and adoptive relationships. Conducts training programs to teach research and recording techniques of family history and genealogical data.

Kansas Genealogical Society
Villager Square Mall-2601 Central
PO Box 103
Dodge City, KS 67801
(316) 225-1951
FOUNDED: 1958.

Kansas Institute for African-American and Native-American Family
  History
5757 Rowland Street
Kansas City, KS 66104-2843

Kansas Council of Genealogical Societies
PO Box 3858
Topeka, KS 66608-6858

Kentucky (www.state.ky.us)

Kentucky Genealogical Society
PO Box 153
Frankfort, KY 40602
(502) 223-7541
FOUNDED: 1973. Individuals interested in the study of Kentucky
genealogy. Maintains library.

Kentucky Historical Society
PO Box 1792
Frankfort, KY 40602-1792

Louisiana (www.state.la.us)

Comite Des Archives de la Louisiana (CAL)
PO Box 44370
Baton Rouge, LA 70804
(504) 387-4264
FOUNDED: 1978. Promotes the maintaining of archives, historic
preservation, and genealogical research in Louisiana.

Genealogical Research Society of New Orleans (GRSNO)
PO Box 51791
New Orleans, LA 70151
(504) 581-3153

FOUNDED: 1960. Serves individuals, libraries, and universities promoting the study of genealogy in the Mississippi Gulf Coast region of the United States.

Creole-American Genealogical Society
PO Box 3215, Church St. Sta.
New York, NY 10008
FOUNDED: 1983. Promotes Creole-American genealogical research. Dedicated to the social, psychological, historical, and genealogical needs of the biracial person. Provides family trees.

Maine (www.state.me.us)

Maine Genealogical Society
PO Box 221
Farmington, ME 04938-0221

Maine Historical Society
485 Congress Street
Portland, ME 04101
(207) 774-1822
FOUNDED: 1822. Individuals interested in preserving the history of Maine. Operates Maine History Gallery and Wadsworth Longfellow House. Holds public programs and conducts charitable activities.

Maryland (www.state.md.us)

Maryland Genealogical Society
201 West Monument Street
Baltimore, MD 21201

Massachusetts (www.state.ma.us)

Massachusetts Society of Genealogists
PO Box 215
Ashland, MA 01721

Massachusetts Genealogical Council
PO Box 5393
Cochituate, MA 01778
Serves as frontline advocate to the genealogical community. Monitors legislation affecting public access to historical and current demographic records.

Michigan (www.state.mi.us)

Michigan Genealogical Council
PO Box 80953
Lansing, MI 48908-0953

Minnesota (www.state.mn.us)

Minnesota Genealogical Society
PO Box 16069
St. Paul, MN 55116-0069
(612) 645-3671
FOUNDED: 1969. Amateur and professional family historians. Promotes interest in genealogy and teaches members and others the procedures for tracing their family history. Provides assistance to individuals conducting a specific nationality research.

Mississippi (www.state.ms.us)

Historical and Genealogical Association of Mississippi
618 Avalon Road
Jackson, MS 39206

Mississippi Genealogical Society
PO Box 5301
Jackson, MS 39296
(601) 924-1735
Individuals with an interest in history and genealogy. Gathers, preserves, and disseminates genealogical and historical information.

Missouri (www.state.mo.us)

Missouri State Genealogical Association
PO Box 833
Columbia, MO 65205-0833
(816) 747-9330

State Historical Society of Missouri
1020 Lowry Street
Columbia, MO 65201-7298
(314) 882-7083
FOUNDED: 1898. Individuals interested in preserving the history of Missouri and the western United States. Annual meeting each fall.

Mississippi County Genealogical Society
PO Box 5
Charleston, MO 63834
Monthly meeting on the third Thursday each month.

Montana (www.state.mt.us)

Montana State Genealogical Society
PO Box 555
Chester, MT 59522

Nebraska (www.state.ne.us)

Nebraska State Genealogical Society
PO Box 5608
Lincoln, NE 68505
(402) 266-8881

Nevada (www.state.nv.us)

Nevada State Genealogical Society
PO Box 20666
Reno, NV 89515

New Hampshire (www.state.nh.us)

New Hampshire Society of Genealogists
PO Box 2316
Concord, NH 03302-2316
(603) 432-8137
FOUNDED: 1978. Persons interested in genealogy. Educates the public about New Hampshire and regional genealogy, and offers assistance in conducting genealogical research.

New Jersey (www.state.nj.us)

Genealogical Society of New Jersey
PO Box 1291
New Brunswick, NJ 08903
(908) 356-6920

New Jersey Historical Society
230 Broadway
Newark, NJ 07104

New Mexico (www.state.nm.us)

Hispanic Genealogical Research Center of New Mexico
1331 Juan Tabo NE
Albuquerque, NM 87112-0000

New Mexico Genealogical Society
PO Box 8283
Albuquerque, NM 87198-8283
(505) 828-2514
Promotes genealogical research. Locates, restores, preserves, and disseminates genealogical information.

Hidalgos of New Mexico
c/o James Hugo Cabeza de Vaca
3310 Tyrone
El Paso, TX 79925
(915) 594-1648
FOUNDED: 1988. Direct descendants of New Mexico's conquerors and first settlers. Encourages genealogical investigations among New Mexican Hispanics.

New York (www.state.ny.us)

New York Genealogical and Biographical Society
122 E. 58th Street
New York, NY 10022-1939
(212) 755-8532
FOUNDED: 1869. To discover, procure, preserve, research, and perpetuate information and items relating to genealogy, biography, and family history, especially of the state of New York. Publishes compiled genealogy and source material for genealogists and historians. Library is open to the public.

Heritage Institute of Ellis Island
19 E. 48th St., Ste. 503
New York, NY 10017
(212) 308-9580
FOUNDED: 1982. Seeks to foster and promote public awareness of
Ellis Island. Offers research and educational programs. Developing
the American Family Immigration History Center,™ a database of
historic data on the 17 million immigrants processed at Ellis Island.

North Carolina (www.state.nc.us)

North Carolina Genealogical Society (NCGS)
PO Box 1492
Raleigh, NC 27602
FOUNDED: 1974. Serves all interested persons. Promotes ge-
nealogical research and the collection, preservation, and use of
archival material. Provides network for the exchange of information.

North Carolina Society of Historians
PO Box 848
Rockingham, NC 28379
(919) 997-6641
Professional and nonprofessional historians organized for fellow-
ship and the study of state history and genealogy.

Order of First Families of North Carolina
PO Box 8605
Rocky Mount, NC 27804-1605

North Dakota (www.state.nd.us)

State Historical Society of North Dakota
612 East Boulevard Avenue
Bismark, ND 58505-0830

Ohio (www.state.oh.us)

Delaware County Historical Society
157 E. William Street
PO Box 317
Delaware, OH 43015-0317
(614) 369-3831
FOUNDED: 1938. Serves individuals and families. Collects, preserves, and disseminates local genealogical material and historical memorabilia. Maintains museum and supports local activities.

Ohio Genealogical Society
34 Sturges Ave.
PO Box 2625
Mansfield, OH 44906-0625
(419) 522-9077
FOUNDED: 1959. Genealogists, historians, libraries, and other interested individuals from throughout the United States. Promotes genealogical research and the preservation of historical records in Ohio. Facilitates the exchange of ideas and information. Sponsors educational programs on family lineage in Ohio. Conducts charitable activities.

Michigan Chapter of the Ohio Genealogical Society
30500 Springland Dr.
Farmington Hills, MI 48334
(810) 477-3956
Promotes Ohio genealogy.

Oklahoma (www.state.ok.us)

Oklahoma Genealogical Society
PO Box 12986
Oklahoma City, OK 73157

Sand Creek Massacre Descendants Trust
PO Box 427
Anadarko, OK 73005-0427
(405) 247-2223
FOUNDED: 1949. Individuals with a bloodline to those victimized in the November 29, 1864 Sand Creek Massacre of Cheyenne and Arapaho Indians. Seeks a redress of Article 6 of the 1865 Little Arkansas River Treaty. Supports economic development in the surrounding communities, not only in Oklahoma but across the United States. Assists the disadvantaged with food, clothing, and payment of utility bills.

Oregon (www.state.or.us)

Genealogical Council of Oregon
PO Box 628
Ashland, OR 97520

Oregon Genealogical Society
PO Box 10306
Eugene, OR 97440-2306
(503) 746-7924

Pennsylvania (www.state.pa.us)

Genealogical Society of Pennsylvania
1305 Locust St.
Philadelphia, PA 19107-5405
(215) 545-0391
FOUNDED: 1892. A non-profit organization of genealogical researchers in Pennsylvania and the Delaware Valley area of Delaware and New Jersey. Collects and preserves genealogical records. Conducts abstracting, indexing, and microfilming of newspapers and records. Annual conference and monthly program meeting.

Colonial Society of Pennsylvania
215 S. 16th St.
Philadelphia, PA 19102
(215) 735-1525
FOUNDED: 1896. Male lineal descendants of any colonial settler who settled in North America before 1700. Collects and preserves records and documents relating to the early history of the United States.

Historical Society of Pennsylvania
1300 Locust St.
Philadelphia, PA 19107
(215) 732-6200
FOUNDED: 1824. Individuals interested in the history and genealogy of Pennsylvania, the original 13 colonies, and surrounding states. Sponsors exhibits, lectures, and other educational programs. Annual Genealogy and Family History Workshop meeting, usually held in the fall.

Genealogical Society of Southwestern Pennsylvania
PO Box 894
Washington, PA 15301-0894
FOUNDED: 1971. Individuals interested in preserving the genealogy of southwestern Pennsylvania. Conducts genealogical research. Monthly meeting second Sunday of the month, except August.

Rhode Island (www.state.ri.us)

Rhode Island Genealogical Society
PO Box 433
Greenville, RI 02828

South Carolina (www.state.sc.us)

South Carolina Genealogical Society
PO Box 492
Columbia, SC 29202-0492

South Carolina Historical Society
100 Meeting Street
Charleston, SC 29401

South Dakota (www.state.sd.us)

South Dakota Genealogical Society
124 Gilley Ave. S.
Brookings, SD 57006

Tennessee (www.state.tn.us)

Lincoln County Genealogical Society
1508 W. Washington St.
Fayetteville, TN 37334
(615) 433-5991

Tennessee Genealogical Society
PO Box 111249
Memphis, TN 38111
(901) 327-3273

Middle Tennessee Genealogical Society
PO Box 190625
Nashville, TN 37219-0625

Texas (www.state.tx.us)

Texas State Genealogical Society
Rte. 4, Box 56
Sulphur Springs, TX 75482
(903) 885-3523
FOUNDED: 1960.

Daughters of the Republic of Texas
510 E. Anderson Ln.
Austin, TX 78752
(512) 339-1997
FOUNDED: 1891.

Utah (www.state.ut.us)

Family History Department of the Church of Jesus Christ of Latter-
   Day Saints
50 E. North Temple Street
Salt Lake City, UT 84150
(801) 240-2331
FOUNDED: 1894. A department of the Church of Jesus Christ of
Latter-day Saints (Mormon church). Promotes local and family history
(genealogical) research; gathers microfilms and preserves genealogical
data, with 200 projects in 40 countries; accredits genealogical researchers. Maintains 2,000 family history centers in 60 countries.

Genealogical Society of Utah
35 Northwest Temple Street
Salt Lake City, UT 84150

Utah Genealogical Association
PO Box 1144
Salt Lake City, UT 84110
Contains academic information

Vermont (www.state.vt.us)

Middletown Springs Historical Society
On the Green
Middletown Springs, VT 05757
(802) 235-2376
FOUNDED: 1970. Individuals interested in preserving the history
of Middletown Springs, Vermont. Acts as research center. Researches genealogy and maintains listing of cemetery inscriptions.

Vermont Historical Society
109 State Street
Montpelier, VT 05609-0901

Virginia (www.state.va.us)

Genealogical Research Institute of Virginia
PO Box 29178
Richmond, VA 23242-0178

Virginia Genealogical Society
5001 W. Broad St., No 115
Richmond, VA 23230-3023
(804) 285-8954

Virginia Beach Genealogical Society
PO Box 62901
Virginia Beach, VA 23466-2901

Washington (www.state.wa.us)

Washington State Genealogical Society
PO Box 1422
Olympia, WA 98507-1422

West Virginia (www.state.wv.us)

West Virginia Genealogical Society and Library
5238A Elk River Road (Rt. 119)
Elkview, WV 25071
(304) 965-1179

Wisconsin (www.state.wi.us)

State Historical Society of Wisconsin (SHSW)
816 State St.
Madison, WI 53706-1488
(608) 264-6400
FOUNDED: 1846. Promotes wider appreciation of the history of Wisconsin. Maintains state historical museum and archives.

Wisconsin State Genealogical Society
2109 20th Ave.
Monroe, WI 53566
(608) 325-2609
FOUNDED: 1939. Persons interested in Wisconsin genealogy; libraries and organizations with genealogical collections.

Wyoming (www.state.wy.us)

Kemmerer Wyoming State Family History Library
Antelope & 3rd West
Kemmerer, Wyoming 83101
(307) 877-6821

Casper Wyoming Family History Center
3931 W 45th (Wolf Creek Subdivision)
Casper, Wyoming 82604
(307) 234-3326

INTERNATIONAL RESOURCES

WHERE IN THE WORLD?

The bloodlines of mankind begin in Africa, but the African presence is scattered throughout the globe. A myriad of ancestral relationship charts can be drawn from Africa.

I met Tania, a New Zealander, during her family tour of the United States, and her family's story is particularly romantic and fascinating. Her great grandfather was a merchant seaman of African descent from Antigua. While on shore leave in New Zealand, he got involved in a brawl and found himself in jail for the night. His ship set sail the next morning without him, stranding him. He made New Zealand his home and married a Maori princess who abandoned her royal family to be with the man she loved. The princess and the seaman went on to have a happy, idiosyncratic marriage.

Tania and her mother discovered a century old cache of correspondence that the seaman had exchanged with his sister in Antigua. Tania and her mother had never met any of their "American" family, but the day finally came when Tania's mother took a trip from New Zealand to the Caribbean. There she visited the family's ancestral town in Antigua, which she discovered in her grandfather's correspondence, not expecting to find anything. However, she asked questions of a shopkeeper, and found that the shopkeeper was a relative. In this way the family connection was reestablished between New Zealand and Central America. It then extended to North America and the United States.

Finding African ancestry in other countries is rarely this easy, but Tania's story captures elements of what is needed to connect to another country.

• Determine the specific point of entry to the country. If you are tracing enslaved Africans in America back to Africa, you must know where the slave ship docked in the United States. If you have come this far, you probably have an estimated year of the transport.

• Identify the slave ship used to transport your ancestor. This can be done through captain's log books, personal diaries, auction records, and maritime records. Consult Elizabeth Donnan's 18th-century four-volume set of research *Documents Illustrative of the History of the Slave Trade to America*. Donnan's extensive list of names of ships, ship owners, slave purchases, slave sales, and slave names is available in most archives and libraries dedicated to African-American history. It is conceivable that such lists could be used to track Africans transported to the ports of Rhode Island, South Carolina, and Virginia, the most active slave-trading ports.

• Determine what stops the ship may have made between Africa and the Americas. Rarely did a slave ship transport Africans from a single nation or tribe, and not every enslaved African was brought directly to colonial America. You may find references to men, women, and children documented as being from one nation when they were really from another. The ships traveled the coast of Africa trading wares—nuts, fruit, gold, and Black slaves. They also stopped and traded among the populations of Central and South

America, Cuba, Jamaica, and the West Indies. And many Africans from the same family or tribe were separated in transactions among the ship's own crew. Again, the obstacle most difficult to overcome in Black genealogy is facing you—tracing an individual whose individuality has been stripped.

• Identify the tribal nation from which your ancestor was sold or kidnapped. Because names given to the countries and natives of Africa have evolved, this must be done for both "ancient" and "contemporary" Africa.

• Locate and connect with an African historian, scholar, or griot to piece together "the story" of a tribe or a specific ancestor.

Tracking your ancestor back to Africa is going to be nothing short of miraculous. But dogged persistence and creativity will pay off. Most of the information you need can be gathered by letter writing. But your presentation of "the evidence" must be clearly described, neatly documented, and introduced diplomatically. Unless you are paying an upfront fee for professional genealogy assistance, societies and associations (many of them foreign) are not required to assist you in any way. Make your request for information as doable as possible.

INTERNATIONAL RESOURCES—GENERAL

Family History Department of the Church of Jesus Christ of Latter-Day Saints
50 E. North Temple
Salt Lake City, UT 84150
PH: (801) 240-2331
FX: (801) 240-5551
FOUNDED: 1894. Also known as the Genealogical Society of

Utah. Unsurpassed in its genealogical records in size, scope, and access. As a department of the Church of Jesus Christ of Latter-day Saints (Mormon church), the Family History Center™s (FHCs) provide access to local and family history (genealogical) research; gather microfilms and preserve genealogical data, with 200 projects in 40 countries. Maintains 2,000 FACs in 60 countries. Computerized services include several databases available on CD-ROM: Family-Search: Ancestral File; FamilySearch: International Genealogical Index; FamilySearch: Library Catalog; FamilySearch: Social Security Death Index. Publishes research outlines periodically.

International Genealogy Consumer Organization (IGCO)
4329 S. Stafford Way
West Valley City, UT 84119
FOUNDED: 1980. Purpose is to ensure ethical genealogical research by registering qualified genealogists who have agreed to IGCO's International Professional Code of Ethics. Disseminates information to the public. Publishes the *International List of Registered Genealogists*.

International Society for British Genealogy and Family History
PO Box 3115
Salt Lake City, UT 84110-3115
(801) 240-4314
FOUNDED: 1979. Serves professional and amateur genealogists. Strives to foster interest in the genealogy and family history of persons of British descent, improve U.S.-British relations, increase the educational opportunities and knowledge of members and the public, and encourage preservation of historical records and access to records.

Society for Historical Archaeology
PO Box 30446
Tucson, AZ 85751
PH: (602) 886-8006
FX: (602) 886-0182
FOUNDED: 1967. Serves archaeologists, historians, anthropologists and ethnohistorians and other individuals and institutions with an interest in historical archaeology or allied fields. Aim is to bring together persons interested in studying specific historic sites, manuscripts, and published sources, and to develop generalizations concerning historical periods and cultural dynamics as they emerge through the techniques of archaeological excavation and analysis. Main focus is the era beginning with the exploration of the non-European world by Europeans, and geographical areas in the Western Hemisphere, but it also considers Africa, Oceania, and Asian archaeology during relatively late periods.

AFRICANS IN AMERICA

Poring over the annals of slave ships and slave bills of sale is often a stomach turning and contemptible chore. It is not something that everyone can do. However, if you are tenacious and persist, you can probably trace an ancestor abroad, even to Africa.

By now you are aware that there are many societies and resources to assist you in your genealogical efforts. However, before you reach out to an international agency, make sure you have done your homework and exhausted every other means of acquiring the information. Why do you believe this organization can help you? What documentary evidence are you providing for the agency to reference—cargo manifest, passenger list, oral history? Provide neat annotated copies of your research. Include as much helpful detail as possible—names, ages, dates, seasons. You may have to research the postal currency for the country so you can include a SASE with your query. Plan for everything. Make it as painless as possible to assure the likelihood of a response.

AFRICANS IN OTHER LANDS

The presence and influence of Africans throughout the world was not always publicly acknowledged, but it wasn't hidden, either. There are ancient and current African descendants in Russia, Asia, Australia, Spain, and England. The great 19th-century Russian poet, Alexander Pushkin, proudly embraced his great-grandmother's African heritage. Today, the journalist and Russian celebrity, Yelenga Khanga, relates the story of her grandparents, a black agronomist and a Polish Jewish immigrant, who fled to the Soviet Union in the 1930s to escape racial intolerance. The daughter of this union married a Zanzibari leader and their daughter is Yelenga Khanga. Born in Russia, Khanga writes about her Russian/African/Polish roots in her family history, *Soul to Soul: The Story of a Black Russian American Family 1865-1992.*

Africans and African-Americans are a people who share in thousands and millions of individual pedigree stories—patches of wisdom and history interwoven into an historic crazy quilt of history.

"De price of yo' hat ain't de measure of yo' brain."
—African-American proverb

SELECTED INTERNATIONAL RESOURCES—BY CONTINENT AND COUNTRY

Africa

African-American Family History Association
PO Box 115268
Atlanta, GA 30310
Newsletter, project, meetings.

Afro-American Genealogical & Historical Society of Chicago
PO Box 37-7651
Chicago, IL 60637
Newsletter, workshops.

Association of African Universities
PO Box 5744, Accra-North
Accra, Ghana
PH: (21) 663281
FX: (21) 664293
Prof. Donald E. U. Ekong, Secretary General
FOUNDED: 1967. Languages include Arabic, English, French. Representatives of universities in 39 countries. Promotes the increased use of African languages. Although primarily an exchange for scholars and professors in universities, provides reader services. Publishes *Who's Who in African Universities*.

Egypt

American Coptic Association
PO Box 9119
Jersey City, NJ 07304

Inter Exchanges Assistance
7, rue du Bois des Trentaines

Le Rocreuil
Eterville
F-14930 Maltot, France
PH: (31)266271
Mr. Ignace Houndole, President
FOUNDED: 1987. Serves individuals in African and European countries interested in organizing trips for the purposes of recreation and cultural exchange, including trips to museums, excursions to villages, and participation in local life to enhance an authentic experience of culture.

Liberia

The Republic of Liberia was originally founded as a refuge for freed African slaves from the United States. The descendants of those freed slaves governed from 1878 to 1980. A succession of military coups has disrupted the government as rival factors fight for government control. Since April 1996 renewed violence has brought the deaths of almost 200,000 civilians. At this writing Liberia and other nations are in civil unrest. It is doubtful that university, diplomatic, and journalistic resources are approachable for genealogical pursuit.

Nigeria

Office of the Embassy
2204 R Street
Washington, DC 20008

World Pan African Movement
2-8 Calcutta Crescent, Gate 4
PO Box 610, Apapa
Lagos, Nigeria
Promotes unity among individuals of African descent worldwide. Works to reverse the negative legacy of European colonialism. Seeks to stimulate public interest in African history and culture.

Senegal

Office of the Embassy
2112 Wyoming Ave.
Washington, DC 20008

Sierre Leone

Office of the Embassy
1701 19th Street, NW
Washington, DC 20009

Recommended web site: AfricaGenWeb (www.rootsweb.com/~africagw)

Asia

Amistad Research Center
Tilton Hall
Tulane University
6823 Saint Charles Ave.
New Orleans, LA 70118
PH: (504) 865-5535
Focuses on African-Americans, Native-Americans, Hispanics, and Asian-Americans. Publishes *Amistad Reports*.

British Association of Cemeteries of South Asia
76 Chartfield Ave.
London, England SW15 6HQ
Mr. T. Wilkinson

Hawaii Chinese History Center (HCHC)
111 North King St., Room 410
Honolulu, HI 96817
PH: (808) 521-5948
Publishes *HCHC Newsletter*.

(Recommended web site: AsianGenWebProject
(www.rootsweb.com/~asiagw/)

Russia

Facts OnLine
812 Vista Dr.
Camano Island, WA 98292
PH: (206) 387-8901
Maintains an office in Moscow, providing access to records in Russian archives.

Russian-American Genealogical Archival Service
PO Box 236
Glen Echo, MD 20812

Soviet-American Genealogical Archival Service
National Archives and Records Administration
Office of Public Programs
Seventh and Pennsylvania Ave., NW
Washington, DC 20408

Canada

American-Canadian Genealogical Society
PO Box 668
Manchester, NH 03105

American-French Genealogical Society
PO Box 2113
Pawtucket, RI 02861

Canadian Historical Association
395 Wellington St.
Ottawa, Ontario K1A 0N3

Recommended web site: Canada GenWeb
(www.geocities.com/Heartland/6625/cngenweb.html)

Recommended website: EuroGenWeb
(www.worldgenweb.orgleurogenweb)

Hispania

Amistad Research Center
Tilton Hall
Tulane University
6823 Saint Charles Ave.
New Orleans, LA 70118
PH: (504) 865-5535
Focuses on African-Americans, Native-Americans, Hispanics, Asian-Americans. Publishes *Amistad Reports*.

Apache Genealogy Society
Sierra Vista Public Library
Maria Bishop Room
PO Box 1084
Sierra Vista, AZ 85636-1084
PH: (602) 458-7770
Specializes in how to do Hispanic research. Publishes *The Genealogist*.

Chicano Research Collection
Department of Archives and Manuscripts
Hayden Library
Arizona State University
Tempe, AZ 85287-1006
Focuses on Mexican-American history and Mexican-Americans in the United States.

Chilean Society of History and Geography
Casilla 1386

Correo Central
Santiago, Chile
PH: (2) 6382489
FOUNDED: 1911. Membership, 309. Serves individuals interested in the study of Chilean and Latin American history, geography, archaeology, anthropology, and folklore.

Cuban Genealogical Society
2552 Tamar Dr.
PO Box 2650
Salt Lake, City, UT 84110
Publishes *Revista*.

Genealogical Society of Hispanic America
PO Box 9606
Denver, CO 80209
Publishes *Nuestras Raices Quarterly Journal* and *Nuestras Raices Newsletter* (primarily refers to New Mexico and Colorado).

Recommended web sites:
(Mexico Geo Web (www.rootsweb.com/~mexwgw);

SouthAmGenWeb (www.rootsweb.com/~sthamgw)

9

SPECIALIZED RESOURCES

At some point you are going to need help with your research. We all do. You may need to locate a specific resource, require direction in resolving a unique problem, or want to contact an expert. African-American associations, general genealogical societies, and the online community can assist you with special concerns.

Multi-racial lineage is almost inevitable when doing American genealogy. You may need to approach a Native-American, Hispanic, or Caribbean association for information or guidance. Adoptees have a special genealogical challenge. If you or your relative was adopted, changes in laws and attitudes toward adoption have made new information and resources available, defending the rights of adoptees and birth parents.

Computer and online resources are a special asset to genealogy. After all, the Internet and World Wide Web were designed to help us share information and make connections with strangers. Repositories of data, special interest groups, individual explorers, and how-to tutorials are accessible in the cyber community.

Whether you post your research questions in a letter or on an electronic bulletin board, the same query etiquette applies. Before contacting any outside agency, by letter or electronic query, be certain you know that there is something that the agency can offer. When you approach the professional or dedicated amateur communities for research, be certain you have exhausted all other resources and that you have your information at your fingertips. You should have a definite idea about what you are looking for and be able to communicate that need so another person can understand it. For example, if you have the surname, birthdate, place of birth, and death date of a relative but haven't been able to locate his or her parents, posting a query to a bulletin board or listserver would be a reasonable next step—you are looking to build upon existing information and extend the connection. On the other hand, I have eavesdropped on an incident at a Family History Center™ that may be too typical. A gentleman comes in to use the FHC database. He explains to the librarian that he is looking for "Jane Doe" of "Cleveland, Ohio." The librarian was a very patient fellow and asked for more details about Ms. Doe. But the patron was unable to provide a birthdate (or estimated age), death date, social security number, or even an address for his subject. He was frustrated, but his attempt to do research without the most basic planning was the cause of his frustration.

Resources presented in this chapter can be used as starting places, but familiarize yourself with traditional book and document materials made available for beginners. Jumping into a group before you have done your homework risks wasting your own and other people's time, and alienating the very people who could help you.

African-American Historical and Genealogy Associations

Unique information on the Black experience has been gathered in a variety of formats. They are also usually a great place to network and locate the books, periodicals, and narratives that are specific to your search. The complexity of the human genealogical experience combined with the complexity of the Black experience make these associations and services a sanctuary for the African-American researcher. They serve as repositories or pointers to biographical, sociological, statistical, and historical information that would be impossible for an individual to gather alone. Oral histories of former slaves, freeman's records, Black cemeteries, and African pilgrimages are among the specialized tools they offer.

Afro-American Historical and Genealogical Society
PO Box 73086
Washington, DC 20056
(202) 234-5350
FOUNDED: 1977. Serves individuals, libraries, and archives. Encourages scholarly research in Afro-American history and genealogy as it relates to American history and culture. Collects, maintains, and preserves relevant material, which the society makes available for research and publication. Conducts seminars and workshops.

African-American History Association
PO Box 115268
Atlanta, GA 30310
(404) 344-7405
FOUNDED: 1977. Serves persons interested in African-American family history and genealogy. Conducts research programs and tours; maintains speakers bureau.

Kansas Institute for African-American and Native-American Family
   History
5757 Rowland St.
Kansas City, KS 66104

Afro-American Historical and Genealogical Society,
Chicago Chapter
PO Box 438652
Chicago, IL 60643
(312) 821-6473

FOUNDED: 1989. Promotes scholarly research, projects, writing, and publishing that further the study of African-American genealogy, history, and culture.

Research Institute of African and African Diaspora Arts
12 Morley St.
Roxbury, MA 02119
(617) 427-8325
FOUNDED: 1977. Promotes research into African culture as it relates to African-Americans and others of African heritage living outside of Africa.

Schomburg Center for Research in Black Culture
515 Malcolm X Blvd.
New York, NY 10037-1801
(212) 491-2200
FOUNDED: 1926. Promotes scholarly research and has a renowned collection of manuscripts, art and artifacts.

COMPUTERS AND GENEALOGY

In the mid-1990s the Internet exploded with genealogical information. This electronic network proved to be a timesaving resource, providing speed, efficiency, and economy. What used to be known as armchair genealogy can now be described as laptop genealogy. Hundreds of thousands of amateur and professional genealogists, genealogy forums, and resource tools exist in cyberspace. Some resources are provided by respected genealogical providers and others are created by networks of individuals. The quality of the information varies widely in accuracy and significance, but the Internet is a resource you should explore.

Many sources of genealogical information—including Black genealogy—are available via computer. And the electronic community of bulletin boards, mailing lists, newsgroups, and listservers include African-Americans. General resource guides that a few years ago were only available at a specific location are now available from any computer terminal and modem. Specific information for a geographic region or state is only a few keystrokes away, and online periodicals help you stay current with events and issues in genealogy. New resources to uncover the roots of the African-American experience are added with regularity. Major metropolitan libraries and universities are using the Internet to make their collections available to the public, and commercial services provide public records and people-finding services for a fee. Specialized resources, such as the famous collection of The Church of Jesus Christ of Latter-Day Saints, are now accessible via computer. Personal genealogy pages for specific family lines appear on the Internet frequently.

These resources could be one-stop shopping for your genealogy project, but it is important to note that these resources are often only informational and do not contain original records. So, while you cannot tap into the records of the Randolph County, North Carolina Clerk, you may find someone who has documented what the office contains and noted its usefulness. You may also find a distant relative who has already extended the line you are working on.

There isn't a book that can compete with the instructional and informational resources available on the World Wide Web. There are thousands, if not millions, of pages of guides, surname lists, queries, and reports. Updates occur monthly, weekly, or sometimes even daily. Access to many of the printed indexes and catalogs of libraries throughout the world are being made available on the Internet. Electronic forums and chat rooms are replacing the community that was once limited to letter writing and travel.

A solidly established pedigree chart is still your starting point. Examine the Internet to learn what resources are available and where your research may lead, but note that traditional methods of starting a genealogy project still apply: mapping out your family members with identifying demographic and geographic information, interviews with older relatives, and confirmation of research. The stronger your own foundation, the less vulnerable you are to inaccurate or misleading information from others. Always verify and support any information you may get.

If you don't have a computer, many large metropolitan libraries provide access terminals. Current technology also provides Internet hookups via cybercafes and television sets. Using the Internet you can review some excellent how-to advice by people with the same surname, in the same town or with the same problems. You can also review the end result of other genealogical projects—family histories, three dimensional genealogical charts, and family reunion diaries. You can post messages—"I'm looking for descendants of Wes Taylor born 1862 in Fairfield, South Carolina (half-brother Henry Taylor born 1855)." You can answer messages—"If your great-aunt Maranda was born in 1844 in South Carolina, please contact me." You can collect specialized and general genealogy resources from the beginning stages or the most advanced stages of your research.

Software

If you choose to keep your genealogical records in a computer, take a few precautions and ask yourself a few questions first.

1. Do I have enough data for a computer?

2. How much time do I plan to spend on the project—months, years, a lifetime?

3. Are there other family members proficient with the computer and software to continue my work?

4. Am I planning to amass a large amount of information—tracking dozens of names and places?

5. What kind of computer environment am I working in—IBM/PC or MacIntosh?

6. Am I planning to stay with that environment for a while?

7. Are my goals and my software and hardware compatible—can it make charts?

8. Can I modify fields?

One thing your genealogy software program must have is GED-COM capability. GEDCOM works as a software interface and standard that allows you to exchange information in your computer with another computer that may be using different software. This permits sharing and dissemination of information and is especially useful if you are also receiving information from other sources via E-mail. Be sure to run any files you download from other computers or the Internet through a virus protection software.

Computers are common in our everyday lives. But computer users, especially genealogists, vary in skill and passion. You may be a IBM/PC user and the next historian is a Mac user. Sharing information about your family roots is a central reason for doing the research. Let family members know what you are doing so that the database you are building can be shared with others down the line. If you are simply trying to establish a link to another branch of your family, or are just beginning to explore this subject, a simple notebook will be sufficient for your research. Later you may want to expand your research and transfer data to a computerized system.

If you store your information on a computer, look for a computer software program that allows you to enter names, dates, and places in one master file; letting the software file, relate, and create group sheets and charts relating those names and places. Make sure you like the way the program looks on screen and on paper!

An exceptional source on the Internet's World Wide Web for

Black genealogy is Afrigeneas. The site is maintained by Mississippi State University and was established in April 1993. It is a mailing list of genealogical "buddies" focusing on African ancestry. But it also provides some of the best links to genealogical sources for the African-American in the world. The site has amassed some of the best tutorial and bibliographic resources available on African-American family history. Before you participate in Afrigeneas discussions, acquaint yourself with the FAQs (Frequently Asked Questions), General Resources, and Biographical Outline. The FAQs will introduce you to the site and how it works.

The General Resources area includes reliable and useful sources and the Biographical Outline provides a structure for completing an oral history or interview. The outline has been proclaimed one of the best of its kind on the Web. Areas open for discussion in Afrigeneas include Beginning Family Research; Census Records, Culture, History, Location Queries; People & Places Queries; Plantation Records; Records/Events Queries; Resources; Slavery/Enslavement; Surname Queries; and open forums. There is an FTP (File Transfer Protocol) area where archived information, including family history, African-Americans in the military, plantation records, manumission records, and United States records, can be downloaded. One of the most ambitious projects, being undertaken by the W.E.B. DuBois Institute in association with Afrigeneas, is the Slave Trade Database. Information on the 25,000 slave ships of the 16th and 19th century that could be of genealogical value is being compiled and Afrigeneas is monitoring and providing updates on this project. The site is a must see.

Christine's GenealogyWebsite (http://ccharity.com/)

This website is an example of how a quality personal Web page can evolve into a respected resource. This site began as "Christine's" database and repository for information on her "folks": the Russells and the Cobbs of Jackson, Tennessee; the Charitys of Surry and Charles City County, Virginia; the Andersons and the Perkins of Shuqualak, Mississippi; and the Simmons of Detroit, Michigan. Elaborately detailed Tennessee and Virginia sources predominate, but the entries are so exquisitely presented and the links to other databases on the African-American experience (Freedmen's Bureau Records, United States Colored Troops, Native American links, etc.) are so well illustrated that it doesn't matter. The Web Indexes section, listing links to African-American genealogy resources, census information, commercial genealogy links, historical societies, state archives, obituaries, and slave entries in wills are amazing in scope. After you have explored general how-to sites like Afrigeneas, a web site like Christine's Genealogy Website will show you what kind of nitty-gritty resources you can dig into. The scope of this resource is wonderful, even if it's sometimes overwhelming (one link, Top Genealogy Sites, provides a link to 27,000 other links!). Take care to remain focused on your own needs and direction, but take a look.

The Family History Library (*http://www.lds.org*)

This library in Salt Lake City, Utah, is hands down the largest collection of genealogical information in the world. There is no way to accurately describe the extent of its resources. The Family History Library provides some of the best guidance and original data available through its centers. Its databases are updated continuously. Annually an average of 100 million pages of data are added to its collection. The Church of Jesus Christ of Latter-day Saints, which runs the FHL, only recently debuted its official homepage. But there are so many admirers of this resource that hundreds of Internet pages have been dedicated to it. The Internet pages duplicate much of the information available at the local FHC, but you may still need to visit a center to acquire original documents. The FHL's databases, including Ancestral File™, International Genealogical Index, U.S. Social Security Death Index, Military Index, Family History Library Catalog, and Personal Ancestral File™, are unique resources in genealogy. Becoming acquainted with the contents and mechanics of these files will permit you to use them more productively. Because most of the original documents are proprietary, you will still probably need to visit an FHC to request an interlibrary loan of microfilm or microfiche. However, knowing that the pedigree charts and family groups are accessible via the Ancestral File™ before your visit will help you work more efficiently. African-American or Aleut-American, everyone stops here.

The African-American Mosiac: A Library of Congress Resource Guide for the Study of Black History and Culture (http://lcweb.loc.gov/homepage/lchp.html/)

This Web site gives an overview of Library of Congress resources on Blacks in America. It is not a complete listing of the resources available at the Library of Congress and few original documents are accessible here, but it is useful in providing historical context for documents of the African-American experience. The Manuscript Division (http://lcweb.loc.gov/rr/mss/guide/african.html/) contains papers of slaveholders, slave narratives, diaries, and journals and will assist the genealogists in locating relevant information for their research before investing time and money on a trip to Washington, DC.

The National Archives and Records Administration (http://www.nara.gov/)

This site is making a few genealogical records available online. As the keeper of veterans' records and documentary records about individuals in the United States, the NARA is heavily taxed with genealogical queries. The homepage provides a description of NARA's resources, including locations and hours of Regional Archives locations. The Genealogy Page offers an overview of the information available via the NARA. It's a good site to visit before making a trip to Regional Archives or Records Centers.

Providing links to resources can be as much of a service as providing a Web site. There are hundreds of Black resources on the Net with cultural, social, political, historical, and educational emphasis.

African-American Network Resources
(http://blair.library.rhodes.edu/Africahtmls/africanet.html/)

This site out of Rhodes College in Memphis, Tennessee, provides links to some of the most comprehensive African and African-American Internet resources. There are many others, but this particular collection is regularly updated and includes sites with individual biographical information.

Genealogy is a highly individualized pursuit. An approach that may work well for one individual may not work at all for another. Each person brings a different knowledge about the Black experience in addition to highly individual genealogical needs, but sites that monitor and collect some of the more useful collections and resources are of great use to all African-American historians.

Genealogical efforts of non-African-Americans are also a great asset in Black genealogy. Following are some of the most comprehensive.

The National Genealogical Society (http://genealogy.org/NGS/)

The NGS is peerless at compiling resources for genealogical research. The NGS is a respected authority in the field and its homepage contains links to the most reputable sources.

George Archer's NetGuide
(http://www.genealogy.org/~ngs/netguide/welcome.html/)

This self-described work in progress is a scholarly index to genealogical topics on the Internet. There's great information here, but the site requires more than a passing acquaintance with downloading computer files.

Genealogy Resources on the Internet
(http://pmgmac.micro.umn.edu/Genealogy.html/)

This personal page, maintained by P. M. Goblirsch, contains one of the most comprehensive links to genealogical information within all fifty states. A listing of commercial sites that offer fee-based and specialized research is clearly and succinctly presented. It helpfully organizes resources into the following groupings: General, Miscellaneous, Resources in Canada and the United States, Resources in Europe and Australia, Geographical Information, Latter Day Saints (LDS), Commercial Sites, On-Line Periodicals, Library Catalogs and Archives, Bulletin Boards, Mailing Lists, News Groups, Listservers, Genealogy Software, and Other Genealogy Home Pages. Although Ms. Goblirsch is researching German and Swedish ancestry, her sharing of these sources can also be appreciated by descendants of the African diaspora.

Cyndi's List of Genealogy Sites on the Internet
(http://www.cyndislist.com)

This site is a searchable collection of genealogy links. Although not dedicated exclusively to African-American history, the regular updates and category groupings (including African-American) of the site makes it a favorite for targeting research on the Web.

The Genealogy Lady (http://new-jerusalem.com/genealogy/)

At first glance, you may wonder why such a hodgepodge of questions and answers are included here, which has over 65,000 hits per week. But if you look closely, you'll discover that the Genealogy Lady provides some of the most intelligent and thought-provoking responses to genealogy queries. Studying the Q and A about African-Americans and slave records are instructional, but some of the approaches the Lady uses to resolve other queries are also instructional. The Genealogy Lady claims to have traced genealogy lines from today back to Adam.

Everton Publishers (http://www.everton.com/)

Everton has published a genealogical magazine since 1947. Although it is largely a commercial site, there are many free resources available on its homepage. Its Special Genealogical Resources area includes Genealogical Resources From or About Churches, Societies, Ethnic Groups, and Adoptees. Everton also provides a variety of "Genealogical Helpers." At http://www.everton.com/oel-7/lc.htm a concise and lengthy assessment of the Library of Congress: Civil War Sources and the African-American Experience is presented. Adoption Resources links are also investigated.

Almost every genealogical resource links page includes links to resources for adoptees, but this is one activist site that should not be missed if this area is of interest to you.

Open Records for Adult Adoptees (http://www.bastards.org/activism/)
The site provides links to adoption statutes, legislative codes, reform efforts, and an online adoptee library and bookstore.

Roots Web Genealogical Data Cooperative (http://www.rootsweb.com)
Proclaiming to be the oldest and largest genealogy site, this resource compiles an exhaustive amount of genealogical activity and services.

Mailing lists exist to disseminate information on a topic via e-mail. Sign up by sending e-mail to the listserver address and typing "subscribe" in your query and sit back and wait. ROOTS-L is one of the most popular and useful mailing lists. Subscribe to roots-l-request@rootsweb.com; Afrigeneas subscription requests go to list-proc@msstate.edu; and to Genweb at listserv@ucsd.edu.

News groups are similar to forums and mailing lists, but they are divided into geographical groupings. Select from a list the group you wish to participate in. Type the address into your search window, for example, soc.genealogy.misc (general discussion); soc.roots (full of information including information on ROOTS-L); and soc.genealogy.surnames (surname searches).

Homepages exist by the thousands. They are often straightforward sites offering surname searches, special projects, queries, and forums for sharing and preserving information. To find such a site is usually no more difficult than typing in a keyword for an ethnicity (e.g., Puerto Rican, Mexican, Sioux) or surname in combination with the word "genealogy" or "genealogical," using any of the Internet search engines (AltaVista, Yahoo, Excite). Watch the progress of the International Genealogical Society (IIGS™) at htt:www.iigs.org as it unites genealogists from around the world and links their research in multilingual formats.

COMMERCIAL ONLINE SERVICES

Commercial online databases provide access to the Internet and World Wide Web from your home or office, but there are also separate products that provide specialized information. Forums offering guidance, tips, and resources are available on most commercial online services. These exist separately from the Internet and are limited to members of the online service. CompuServe, America Online, and Prodigy are among the largest service providers and all maintain genealogy forums and access to the Internet. Find these forums using a keyword search for GENEALOGY (ROOTS for America Online). All have areas dedicated to Black genealogy.

Commercial online databases of information on individuals are in heavy competition with resources available on the Internet. Many, like Everton Publishers (http:www.everton.com/), are making selected parts of their databases available for free and providing guides and helps for amateur genealogists. Everton provides a card catalog to over 40,000 books, a genealogical dictionary, and online genealogy classes for a fee-based subscription. Such a database is useful for advanced research, but many people at the beginning of their search for lost relatives are using any number of people locator tools for free.

Social Security number searches are the swiftest and most accurate people identifiers available in the United States. Possessing a Social Security number for a relative will expedite the receipt and delivery of documents such as death benefits, pension records, and employment history. The U.S. Social Security Act was established in 1935, and records are available starting in 1936. Since the late 1970s and early 1980s, the Social Security Number has been informally adopted as a national identifier. Today, even infants are assigned numbers before they are two years old. Social Security records won't be fully available until 2008. But for relatives, under extenuating circumstances, the Department of Social Security will forward correspondence. It will not release the address to you directly, and further contact will be at the discretion of the addressee.

The Social Security Administration also provides electronic access to its statistics indirectly. Death records are available via a tape format of 50 million deaths called the Death Master File, which is available for sale to the public via the U.S. Department of Commerce, National Technical Information Service for $1,500 to $6,000. Here's an example of how your membership in an association can work for you. Many of the larger genealogical sources purchase this tape and make it available to their members. The Family History Library also provides free access to the information to anyone. The Social Security Administration experimented with an Internet service that provided Social Security numbers, but removed it after numerous protests. Still, the FAQ site (http://www.ssa.gov/faq_services.html) provides answers to the most common questions relevant to the family historian.

NEXIS-Express (800-843-6476) will perform a search in their electronic database for a cost of approximately $10 per minute—the average call lasts 5 to 7 minutes. The database once contained a Death Index as well as current Social Security information, but it has since been reduced to only death records. It is a major resource of law enforcement, journalism, and legal professionals. If money is not an obstacle, Internet access is not available, and speed is of paramount importance, NEXIS/LEXIS is an excellent resource. However, fees are incurred even if a "no hits" result is found.

With listings for over 100 million residential and business listings, electronic directories such as Switchboard (http://www.switchboard.com) can even feature some of its many reunion stories on its Switchboard Stories page. I was able to reunite a cousin with a long lost friend (twenty years lost) with a Switchboard search. The search went so smoothly I repeated it in several other databases just to confirm the information—much of the information in the databases comes from the same public information sources. Some Web sites provide more features than others (i.e. location maps, e-mail addresses, census and demographic information), but they all work much like a telephone directory. Four11 (http://www.411.com) and BigBook (http://www.bigbook.com) also provide free access to phone and address directories throughout the United States.

Commercial services for genealogy include software and computer services, publishers and booksellers, photography, preservation, maps, and research services. Many of the previously mentioned sites provide excellent links to commercial enterprises, but a site at http://www.gen homepage.com/commercial.html#comersoft provides an attractive grouping of prominent commercial vendors and services.

Telecommunications and the electronic transfer of information is changing and challenging how we communicate and exchange information. The advent of electronic bulletin boards, telephone directories, chat groups, and data transfer is swiftly changing the way genealogy is compiled. Before you can finish reading these descriptions, the resources here will be updated and enhanced; none of this information is static. The volatility of electronic resources is probably its most exciting detail. You may find that a resource has changed just months after you last used it. Use your favorite search engine to expand the resources listed here. Through your involvement with a discussion group or bulletin board, you may be surprised to find a cousin or two working on the same genealogical line. Revisit sites often because the power of the Internet is in its linking and layering of information. If you approach the electronic superhighway with tenacity and care, you may be very excited when you reach your destination.

The Internet provides the gateway to general genealogy resources, geographical information, Latter Day Saints (LDS) resources; commercial sites; on-line periodicals, library catalogs and archives, bulletin boards, mailing lists, news groups, listservers, genealogy software, and other personal genealogy homepages. In the future, our personal telephone records, online writings, video diaries, credit card statements, passport and driving records may be explicit testimonials for our descendants to retrace our steps.

PROFESSIONAL GENEALOGISTS

Professional genealogists can be hired to perform specialized searches, to trace ancestry over longer periods of time, to find missing people, to search records, and to provide other specialized services. Computerized searching and translation of foreign records are professional specialties. However, the fees are high and the results may not be substantially better than what you can find for free or at low cost.

TRAVEL

Black genealogy has also become a business venture for travel agencies. The National Register of Historic Places has identified and described over 800 locations (since December 31, 1993) that reflect the contribution of African-Americans to American history. Sites are continuously being added to this resource. State-by-state breakdowns, which include Black migration patterns and safe houses on the Underground Railroad, are available.

The phenomenon of the "roots" traveler has been keeping the African village of Juffure engaged with its African-American cousins. Even if you can't trace your ancestry back to Africa, a trip to do some "roots" research can be useful in a genealogy project. Travel agencies specializing in Senegal, Gambia, and the Ivory Coast have reported steady business since the late 1970s.

Henderson Travel Services is the "oldest and most experienced full-service minority travel agency." Since 1957, from its main office in Washington, DC, it was the first to design packages touring West African destinations. Visit their Web site at http://www.hend.com/travel.htm or call 202-387-6611 for available tours. Similar services are provided by competing travel and touring agencies. Ask your travel agent about packages.

10

~

FAMILY REUNIONS

There has been a Black family reunion explosion since the 1980s. In 1986, the National Council of Negro Women (NCNW) convened the first of six annual Black Family Reunion Celebrations. Six cities were chosen for their significant contribution to Black history and their significant Black populations: Philadelphia, Cincinnati, Los Angeles, Washington, DC, Memphis, and Atlanta. Over the last ten years, the reunions have attracted over six million people. Even if you're not planning a mega-reunion such as the NCNW, building a family reunion requires serious planning. A family reunion can be a modest at-home dinner or a casual barbecue. But most reunions involve at least two dozen guests. Careful planning will help guarantee a successful event.

First, decide who will be the overall reunion coordinator. This person, or team, will be responsible for developing and executing a reunion plan, sustaining communication, making assignments, and establishing and monitoring deadlines. Invite family members to help in the planning process to ensure that special needs are met. Enlist these helpers to create a master family file with names, addresses, telephone numbers, relations, special interests, and special requests (wheelchair access, dietary restrictions, etc.).

The reunion coordinator will also delegate work among teams or committees. Each team in turn, will have its own coordinator. Ask for volunteers, but don't be shy about making assignments based on a family member's interest or special skill. Teams can work out the details of reunion finances, food, lodging, and entertainment. The finance committee will establish and oversee the budget, reconcile banking fees, disburse monies for scholarships, fees, and expenses. Family assessments and donations should be collected and distributed by this committee. This team could also gather bids from vendors and merchants who may wish to participate in the reunion by donating or discounting goods or services.

Food is essential to any gathering of people, and reunions are no exception. Establish a food and entertainment team. Food can be catered, potluck, or both—just let your guests know when to expect meals and when they will be on their own.

Entertainment can be a simple display of the family photo album or arts and crafts exhibits designed by younger family members. Create a family tree—a three dimensional one! Write a play based on family lore and legend.

A transportation and lodging committee should coordinate with a travel agent to take advantage of travel discounts and group rates on hotels, motels, and airfare. If money is an issue, consider alternative sites such as camp grounds, college dormitories, and the homes of extended family.

Polling the entire family can establish such important business as when to have the gathering, the length of the reunion, the site, activities, and the costs. Some families gather during winter holidays, others prefer the warm summer months when children are free from school and vacation time is plentiful. The more information you have about the expectations of the participants the more comfortable and convenient you can make the reunion.

Information and communications can be handled by committee. Let this team fashion and mail invitations, write a newsletter or update the reunion notebook and family tree. The reunion notebook should contain family members' names, addresses, phone numbers, and any other pertinent information. Looseleaf notebooks allow for the addition or removal of pages, but use sheet protectors to prevent wear and tear on paper.

Recruit reunion liaisons for each branch of the family tree to keep updated with information. This is especially useful if your family reunion involves a hundred people or more. Liaisons will function as reporters and public relations—or family relations—experts. This relieves one person from handling all the questions and phone calls. Rotating this role permits more people to get acquainted and involved with family members they may not have known.

Consider family interests when planning the event, especially the needs of elders and the very young. For example, water sports may be too risky for a lively family reunion with small children and limited skill levels. Yet, that same activity may make an interesting trip for young adults. Senior family members should be showcased and celebrated. This is an opportunity to gather a lot of family history and to acknowledge the contributions of the elders. Select a subject, be it a legendary relative or the old homestead. Grab a video or tape recorder, select a host, and stage your own talk show starring your older relatives.

Finally, be creative in the execution of the reunion. Plan games and activities. Bring out the video camera and update last year's footage. Employ the family artists to create festive invitations and handouts. Make technology work for you—there is usually a computer available. Encourage youngsters to become "reporters" and interview family members. Let them publish their stories in a newsletter or flyer. Your great aunt's photographs can be computer enhanced and would make clever invitations. Don't let traditions get stale and meaningless, inject a little soul whenever you can. Play the music of various periods. Display family photographs with kente or gingham fabric in the background.

Family reunions are a growing tradition in the African-American culture. They are often fun, satisfying, and emotional experiences. They also require a lot of energy and persistence. If you are lucky enough to organize or participate in a reunion, realize that you have attained a goal of connecting with your roots—a living lineage—that many genealogists seek.

11

~~~

METHODOLOGY

African-American genealogy is becoming increasingly popular and accessible. Technology continues to remove such obstacles as time, place, and expense. There is a lot of information out there on Black genealogy in a variety of formats and mediums. Tackling a genealogy project successfully breaks down into planning, recording, and analyzing the known and the unknown.

PLANNING

• Establish goals. Do you want to connect with family members, write a family history, prove celebrity/patriotic heritage, or trace your lineage back to Africa? Keeping your goal in sight will help focus the massive amounts of information you will encounter.

• Complete your individual pedigree chart. Determine what you know and don't know. This is your blueprint for developing further research. Fill out as much of the chart as possible. Birthdates, death dates, and marriage dates are important. Try to go back at least three generations.

• Decide which ancestral line you want to seek additional information about. Make an entry on your log or "to do" sheet about your goals, noting what kind of record may have the information you require. For example, "Find Aunt Jean's birth certificate." So, if you take a break from your research, you will have left a reminder of where you left off. Develop strategy for filling in the blanks— using primary, secondary, or tertiary sources. Primary sources are documents—diaries, journals, and first person accounts; secondary sources are public or government records; and tertiary sources are interviews or third person accounts. Or, you may choose to check the library or Internet for a compilation of research (bibliographies, surname genealogies, family histories) first to learn whether anyone else has work available on this family line.

• Determine your budget. Setting financial limits and restraints keeps your project from getting away from you and becoming expensive and unmanageable. If your primary goal is to search for your family as far back as Africa, then you are going to select information differently than the person who is trying to write a history of a branch of the family in Ohio. Only purchase information that will advance your research toward its goal. You will not necessarily need every record on every relative and their offspring. Nor will you need to purchase every genealogical publication, subscription, or computer innovation available. You will need ready funds for postage, processing fees, and reproduction costs. Set limits within your means. Remember that most of your research can be done from your home using traditional correspondence. Writing for information is still the foundation of genealogical work. You can do a lot of time travel with enough postage and photocopies. Computers are an enhancement of the process. If you have access to a computer and e-mail, the response time for your research queries might be shortened.

• Gather tools for record keeping. They should be simple and portable: paper, looseleaf notebook, pedigree charts and family group sheets, pencil/pen, magnifying glass (to view small print), checks/money orders, small currency and rolls of quarters for copy machines, stationery, SASEs/postage, tape/video recorder, typewriter/computer, printer.

RECORDING

• Solicit information from a genealogical society. Using your own criteria, establish which local or national organization can provide you with access and support; whether through meetings, newsletters, or workshops. These networks can be timesavers—and money savers—as you share and build on your genealogy project. Consider both general and Black genealogical societies for membership. In the early stages you need basic research. Review the associations' goals and fees and make sure they are compatible with yours.

• Identify elders for interviews. Telephone interviews are quick and immediate. Letters from elders provide documents in hand and become their own colorful and charming archive. In-person interviews should be brief and documented. Record interviews with tape, video, and photographs. At the very least, take plentiful notes. Interview senior family members constantly, even when you don't know what you're looking for or what you're listening to. Transcribe interviews immediately to keep the details fresh and vivid. Date and file the tapes and transcription. Assign each relative a number and coordinate all interviews and supporting materials with the relative's family file. Family lore is irreplaceable with the passing of each generation, so move quickly. Funny, embarrassing, tragic, strange, and unimaginable stories add the necessary flavor and personality to a satisfying genealogy project. Seek such stories enthusiastically but use them judiciously, especially if they cannot be supported with other sources.

• Scour family "archives." The family bible, recipe books, trunks, attics, photo albums, medal collections, school albums, programs, obituaries, diaries, scrapbooks, financial records, newsletters, social security records, letters, baptismal certificates, and advertisements are ripe with clues to the past. Visit cemeteries. Follow the documentary footprints.

• Visit and use the goldmine of the Family History Library in Salt Lake City through its centers. Go with the information you have filled in on your pedigree chart, family group sheets, and goal in hand. The Family History Center™ is an excellent place to start looking for compilations. The Family History Center™ provides free access to its index and charges nominal fees for copies and delivery services. These services could run you hundreds of dollars if you tried to replicate their resources on your own.

ANALYZING

• Assess new forms of genealogical information formats and access. Documents that lead or point back to another individual, relationship, activity, or place are of primary interest. The Internet has become a crossroads for millions of inquiries. Study these sources to confirm, refute, or augment the vital statistics data you have in hand. Births, deaths, and marriages provide important familial linkages—the more documentation you have on your ancestors the less likely you will be misled.

• Search for family genealogy in FHC records at every opportunity. Remember that the FHC resources are actively and regularly updated. There are no genealogical minutiae that the FHC deems unworthy of inclusion.

• Use local and state libraries, and cultivate a relationship with the librarian. He or she can be the gateway to advancing your genealogical queries. Keep in mind that the contents of academic, government, and private collections are usually documented in indexes or catalogs available in the local, state, or genealogical library. Check on the feasibility of an interlibrary loan before making trips out of the city or state. Libraries are not just about books.

• Research the geographic history of your family. Knowing local county and state history enriches your knowledge. Collect maps and land surveys of the old homestead from the county clerk's office and historical registers. Date everything.

• Learn to communicate brief, concise expressions of inquiry to relatives, scholars, and government agents. The information you receive from query letters will only be as good as the clarity of your request. Ask a friend or spouse to verify that your request is clear and understandable.

• Use the library or an online database to post queries on electronic bulletin boards or in genealogical publications. For example, "I am collecting information on the relations of Adolphus E. Brown, Black (Negro), born 1910 (Columbia, SC), died 1992 (Brooklyn, NY); married Effie Bailey Brown." Remember to include your contact information.

• Establish a filing system to make your family research easier to retrieve. Assigning a number to each relative as they appear on the pedigree sheet is a popular method. Use folders or a separate file pocket for each document for each individual. Date and source all data collected.

• Attend a genealogy association meeting/workshop/conference. Ask questions, make friends, learn new tactics, approaches, and resources. After assessing one or two associations, select one to join to establish commitment, gather information, and garner camaraderie and fellowship.

• Examine wills, deeds, bank records, and diaries even if you don't know what you're looking for. Serendipity and coincidence play an active role in the genealogical process. Also, make queries to societies—social, fraternal, religious—in which your ancestor may have participated. Their membership directories could be useful in filling out your ancestor's profile.

• Refine your information whenever necessary. When researching the past, new details arise regularly. Remain flexible and open to new information about a relative.

• Keep a printed copy of your research. If you establish an electronic archive, always keep a printed copy of your research on file and purchase virus protection software. Computer viruses can obliterate years of research in an instant.

• Evaluate how close you are to the goal you established. Ask if you are any closer to your goal of reunion, publication, memorial, or ceremony.

• Establish and participate in the tradition of family reunions.

• Write and publish your family history. Donate copies of your completed family history to the FHC, the library, the local college or university, including any updates and corrections.

• Commission or create a family chart. Even if you are not at the end of your research, a lovingly rendered pedigree chart can be inspirational. Use it as a guide but don't feel overly concerned with filling it out completely. It can be updated every other year.

• Cherish the color and flavor of your family story. Especially for the African-American, it is a bittersweet reflection of survival, triumph, and striving.

• Remember that genealogy is not just about digging up roots but also learning to bloom where you're planted.

12

WORKSHEETS

This chapter contains many of the genealogical record keeping tools mentioned throughout the book: the pedigree chart, the family chart, and census forms from the available census from 1790 to 1920. Make copies to use as worksheets and keep these forms in place to use as master copies. They can be enlarged and reproduced to use in your genealogical project.

PEDIGREE CHART. Illustrates your "line" of ancestry or lineage. This is where you begin entering information about yourself and your family. Make a copy of the form. In the upper right-hand corner, number the first chart "1." On the mid left-hand side, where the numeral 1 rests on a line, write your full name, birthdate, spouse, etc. Your father belongs on the line numbered "2." Note that the male is always on an even number. This helps differentiate gender even if names are not distinctively masculine or feminine. Here is where you begin to build and layer the people, dates, and places that you need to move your research forward.

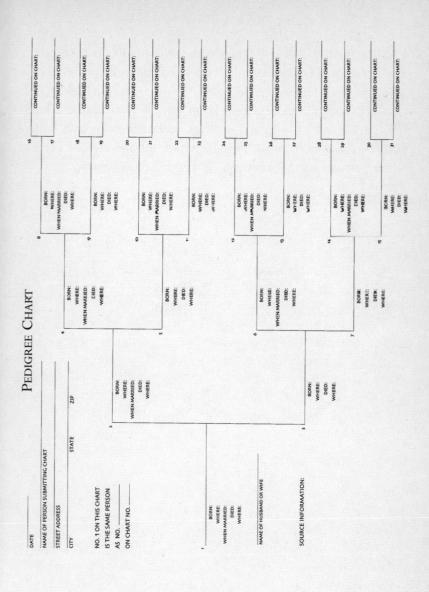

PEDIGREE CHART

DATE _____

NAME OF PERSON SUBMITTING CHART _____

STREET ADDRESS _____

CITY _____ STATE _____ ZIP _____

NO. 1 ON THIS CHART
IS THE SAME PERSON
AS NO. _____
ON CHART NO. _____

1
BORN:
WHERE:
WHEN MARRIED:
DIED:
WHERE:

NAME OF HUSBAND OR WIFE _____

SOURCE INFORMATION:

2
BORN:
WHERE:
WHEN MARRIED:
DIED:
WHERE:

3
BORN:
WHERE:
DIED:
WHERE:

4
BORN:
WHERE:
WHEN MARRIED:
DIED:
WHERE:

5
BORN:
WHERE:
DIED:
WHERE:

6
BORN:
WHERE:
WHEN MARRIED:
DIED:
WHERE:

7
BORN:
WHERE:
DIED:
WHERE:

8
BORN:
WHERE:
WHEN MARRIED:
DIED:
WHERE:

9
BORN:
WHERE:
DIED:
WHERE:

10
BORN:
WHERE:
WHEN MARRIED:
DIED:
WHERE:

11
BORN:
WHERE:
DIED:
WHERE:

12
BORN:
WHERE:
WHEN MARRIED:
DIED:
WHERE:

13
BORN:
WHERE:
DIED:
WHERE:

14
BORN:
WHERE:
WHEN MARRIED:
DIED:
WHERE:

15
BORN:
WHERE:
DIED:
WHERE:

16 CONTINUED ON CHART:

17 CONTINUED ON CHART:

18 CONTINUED ON CHART:

19 CONTINUED ON CHART:

20 CONTINUED ON CHART:

21 CONTINUED ON CHART:

22 CONTINUED ON CHART:

23 CONTINUED ON CHART:

24 CONTINUED ON CHART:

25 CONTINUED ON CHART:

26 CONTINUED ON CHART:

27 CONTINUED ON CHART:

28 CONTINUED ON CHART:

29 CONTINUED ON CHART:

30 CONTINUED ON CHART:

31 CONTINUED ON CHART:

FAMILY GROUP SHEET(S). Consist of more details about a particular family. These sheets are all gathered by family name. For example in the Mary Adelaide Jones chart there is a notation "See: Cook Family" for more details about John Francis Cook, III and Charles Chaveau Cook. A genealogy record may contain both a family group sheet and a pedigree chart for the Cooks. Here is where you can see that neatness and organization counts.

FAMILY GROUP RECORD

HUSBAND _____

OCCUPATIONS: _____

BORN: _____ PLACE: _____
CHRISTENED: _____ PLACE: _____
MARRIED: _____ PLACE: _____
DIED: _____ PLACE: _____
BURIED: _____ PLACE: _____
HUSBAND'S FATHER _____ HUSBAND'S MOTHER _____
HUSBAND'S OTHER WIVES _____

WIFE _____

OCCUPATIONS: _____

BORN: _____ PLACE: _____
CHRISTENED: _____ PLACE: _____
DIED: _____ PLACE: _____
BURIED: _____ PLACE: _____
WIFE'S FATHER _____ WIFE'S MOTHER _____
WIFE'S OTHER HUSBANDS _____

CHILDREN

SEX M/F	GIVEN NAMES SURNAME	WHEN BORN DAY MONTH YEAR	WHERE BORN TOWN	COUNTY	STATE/COUNTY	DATE OF FIRST MARRIAGE	FIRST SPOUSE	WHEN DIED D / M / Y
1								
2								
3								
4								
5								
6								
7								
8								
9								
10								

OTHER MARRIAGES: _____

SOURCE INFORMATION: _____

RELATIONSHIP CHART. A smart tool produced by Emily Croom in *Unpuzzling Your Past*. With this guide you determine how you are related to someone else. For example, suppose you and I have a common ancestor. We have determined that I am a great great grandchild (line 4, side) of this ancestor and you are a great-great-great grandchild (line 5, top). Moving down column 5 and across row 4, at the meeting point we are 3rd cousins once removed. Here's a fun addition to the family reunion activity sheet.

RELATIONSHIP CHART

	1	2	3	4	5	6	7	8	9
COMMON ANCESTOR	SON / DAU.	GRANDSON	GREAT-GRANDSON	G-G GRANDSON	G-G-G GRANDSON	4G GRANDSON	5G GRANDSON	6G GRANDSON	7G GRANDSON
1 — SON / DAU.	BRO / SIS.	NEPHEW / NIECE	GRAND NEPHEW	GREAT GRAND NEPHEW	G-G GRAND NEPHEW	G-G-G GRAND NEPHEW	4G GRAND NEPHEW	5G GRAND NEPHEW	6G GRAND NEPHEW
2 — GRANDSON	NEPHEW / NIECE	1ST COUSIN	1 COU 1 R	1 COU 1 R	1 COU 3 R	1 COU 4 R	1 COU 5 R	1 COU 6 R	1 COU 7 R
3 — GREAT GRANDSON	GRAND NEPHEW	1 COU 1 R	2ND COUSIN	2ND COU 1 R	2 COU 2 R	2 COU 3 R	2 COU 4 R	2 COU 5 R	2 COU 6 R
4 — G-G GRANDSON	GREAT GRAND NEPHEW	1 COU 2 R	2 COU 1 R	3RD COUSIN	3 COU 1 R	3 COU 2 R	3 COU 3 R	3 COU 4 R	3 COU 5 R
5 — G-G-G GRANDSON	GG GRAND NEPHEW	1 COU 3 R	2 COU 2 R	3 COU 1 R	4TH COUSIN	4 COU 1 R	4 COU 2 R	4 COU 3 R	4 COU 4 R
6 — 4G GRANDSON	3G GRAND NEPHEW	1 COU 4 R	2 COU 3 R	3 COU 2 R	4 COU 1 R	5TH COUSIN	5 COU 1 R	5 COU 2 R	5 COU 3 R
7 — 5G GRANDSON	4G GRAND NEPHEW	1 COU 5 R	2 COU 4 R	3 COU 3 R	4 COU 2 R	5 COU 1 R	6TH COUSIN	6 COU 1 R	6 COU 2 R
8 — 6G GRANDSON	5G GRAND NEPHEW	1 COU 6 R	2 COU 5 R	3 COU 4 R	4 COU 3 R	5 COU 2 R	6 COU 1 R	7TH COUSIN	7 COU 1 R
9 — 7G GRANDSON	6G GRAND NEPHEW	1 COU 7 R	2 COU 6 R	3 COU 5 R	4 COU 4 R	5 COU 3 R	6 COU 2 R	7 COU 1 R	8TH COUSIN

ABBREVIATIONS

BRO = BROTHER

SIS = SISTER

DAU = DAUGHTER

COU = COUSIN

R = REMOVED (GENERATION REMOVED)

G-G = GREAT-GREAT

GRANDSON = GRANDSON OR GRANDDAUGHTER

SON = SON OR DAUGHTER

NEPHEW = NEPHEW OR NIECE

The chart may be extended in either direction for identifying more distant relationships.

CENSUS FORMS. Provided to acquaint you with the format and for you to copy and use as worksheets. Census microfilm consists of hundreds of miniature versions of these forms connected on a microfilm reel or microfiche sheet. You can make copies of these forms on which to transfer your information. Make several copies because you will be using more than a few for each year. Of course, you will be able to have copies made using a microfilm reader and printer, but the quality of the copies will vary. Make copies of these forms and complete them as information is acquired.

1790 CENSUS – UNITED STATES

State _____ Call No. _____

County	City	Page	Head of Family	Free White Males 16 & up incl. head of families	Free White Males Under 16	Free White Females Incl. head of family	All Other Persons	Slaves

1800 - 1810 CENSUS – UNITED STATES

State _____ County _____ City _____ Call No. _____

Page	Head of Family	Free White Males					Free White Females					All Others	Slaves	Remarks
		Under 10	10-16	16-26	26-45	Over 45	Under 10	10-16	16-26	26-45	Over 45			

1820 CENSUS – UNITED STATES

State _____ County _____ City _____ Call No. _____

Page	Head of Family	Free White Males						Free White Females					Foreigners not naturalized	Agriculture	Commerce	Manufactures	Free Colored	Slaves	Remarks
		Under 10	10-16	16-18	16-26	26-45	45 and over	Under 10	10-16	16-26	26-45	45 and over							

1830 - 1840 CENSUS – UNITED STATES

State ——— County ——— City ——— Call No. ———

Page	Head of Family	Free White Males														Free White Females														Slaves	Free Colored	Foreigners Not Naturalized
		Under 5	5-10	10-15	15-20	20-30	30-40	40-50	50-60	60-70	70-80	80-90	90-100	Over 100		Under 5	5-10	10-15	15-20	20-30	30-40	40-50	50-60	60-70	70-80	80-90	90-100	Over 100				

1850 CENSUS

UNITED STATES

State _____ County _____ Township _____ Town _____ Call No. _____

Page	Dwelling Number	Family Number	Names	Age	Sex	Color	Occupation, etc.	Value-Real Estate	Birthplace	Married within year	School within year	Cannot read or write	Enumeration Date	Remarks

1860 CENSUS UNITED STATES

State _____ County _____ Town / Township _____ P.O. _____ Call No. _____

Page	Dwelling No.	Family No.	Names	Age	Sex	Color	Occupation, etc.	Value – Real Estate	Value– Personal Property	Birthplace	Married in Year	School in Year	Can't Read or Write	Enumeration Date	Remarks

1870 CENSUS – UNITED STATES

State _____ County _____ Township _____ Town _____ P.O. _____ Call No. _____

Page	Dwelling No.	Family No.	Names	Age	Sex	Color	Occupation, etc.	Value – Real Estate	Value – Personal Property	Birthplace	Father Foreign Born	Mother Foreign Born	Month born in Year	School in Year	Can't Read or Write	Eligible to vote	Date of Enumeration

1880 CENSUS – UNITED STATES

State _____ County _____ Town _____ Township _____ Call No. _____

Page	Dwelling No.	Family No.	Names	Color	Sex	Age prior to June 1	Month of birth if born in census year	Relationship to head of house	Single	Married	Widowed	Divorced	Married in census year	Occupation	Miscellaneous information	Cannot read or write	Place of birth	Place of birth of father	Place of birth of mother	Enumeration Date

1900 CENSUS

Microfilm _____
Roll No. _____

State _____
County _____

Town/Township _____ Date _____

Supv. Dist. No. _____ Sheet No. _____
Enum. Dist. No. _____ Page No. _____

LOCATION				NAME	PERSONAL DESCRIPTION											NATIVITY			CITIZENSHIP			OCCUPATION		EDUCATION						
Street	House No.	Dwelling No.	Family No.	of each person whose place of abode on June 1, 1900, was in this family	Relation to head of family	Color	Sex	Month of birth	Year of birth	Age	Single, married, widowed or divorced	No. of years married	Mother of how many children	Number of these children living	Place of birth	Place of birth of father	Place of birth of mother	Year of immigration to U.S.	No. of years in U.S.	Naturalization	Occupation	No. of months of employment	Attended school: months	Can read	Can write	Can speak English	Home owned or rented	Home owned free or mortgaged	Farm or house

1910 Census – United States

State _____ County _____ Township or other Division of County _____

Enumeration Date _____ Roll _____ Sheet _____ Dist. _____

Top Form

LOCATION			NAME	RELATION	PERSONAL DESCRIPTION						BIRTHPLACE				
Line	House number	Number of dwelling house	Number of family	of each person living in this family on April 15, 1910. (Include every person living on April 15, 1910. Omit children born since April 15, 1910.)	Relationship of the person to the head of the family	Sex	Color or race	Age at last birthday	Single, married, widowed, or divorced	Number of yrs. present marr.	Mother of how many children		Place of birth of this person	Place of birth of father of this person	Place of birth of mother of this person
	city or town										Number born	Number now living			
1															
2															
3															
4															
5															
6															
7															
8															

Bottom Form

CITIZENSHIP		OCCUPATION						EDUCATION			OWNERSHIP OF HOME								REMARKS
Line	Year of immigration to US	Naturalized or Alien	Speak English; or, if not, language spoken	Trade or profession or particular kind of work done by person as spinner, salesman, laborer, etc.	General nature of industry, business or establishment in which person works, as cotton mill, dry goods store, farm, etc.	Whether employer, employee, or working on own account.	Out of work on April 15, 1910	Weeks out of work during year 1909	Able to read?	Able to write?	Attended school any time since Sept. 1, 1909	Owner or rented	Owned free or mortgaged	Farm or house	Number of farm schedule	Whether survivor Union, Confederate Army or Navy	Whether blind (both eyes)	Whether deaf or dumb	
1																			
2																			
3																			
4																			
5																			
6																			
7																			
8																			

SHEET # _____ **A**

DEPARTMENT OF COMMERCE-BUREAU OF THE CENSUS

FOURTEENTH CENSUS OF THE UNITED STATES: 1920-POPULATION

STATE _____   SUPERVISOR'S DISTRICT _____

COUNTY _____   ENUMERATION DISTRICT _____

TOWNSHIP OR OTHER DIVISION OF COUNTY _____

NAME OF INCORPORATED PLACE   WARD OF CITY _____

FILM SERIES T 625: ROLL _____ NAME OF INSTITUTION_____

ENUMERATOR _____ ENUMERATED ON THE ___ DAY OF _____ 1920.

PLACE OF ABODE				NAME	REL.	TENURE		PERSONAL DESCRIPTION				CITIZENSHIP			EDUCATION		
Street, avenue, road, etc.	House number or farm.	Number (of) dwelling house in order of visitation.	Number of family in order of visitation.	of each person whose place of abode on January 1, 1920, was in this family. Enter surname first, then given and middle initial if any. Omit children born since January 1, 1920.	Te head of household.	Home owned or rented	If owned, free or mortgaged.	Sex.	Color or race.	Age at last birthday.	Single, married, widowed, or divorced	Year of immigration to the United States.	Naturalized or alien.	If naturalized,year of naturalization.	Attended school any time since 1 Sept. 1919.	Whether able to read.	Whether able to write.
1	2	3	4	5	6	7	8	9	10	11	12	13	14	15	16	17	18
			1														
			2														
			3														
			4														
			5														
			6														
			7														
			8														
			9														
			10														
			11														
			12														
			13														
			14														
			15														

FILM READ AT _____

BY _____ DATE _____

BIBLIOGRAPHY

Reading is required for all genealogists—amateur and professional. Your research will be enhanced when you stretch your knowledge because you will know more about the motivations and influences affecting an ancestor in a given time, place, or occupation. Sometimes you will need to look up from your charts and notes—maybe even put them away for a while—and take a break or pursue a new vision. That may be the time to pick up a book to help bring that vision into focus. Some books are considered classics in African-American history and genealogy. You can choose to go back and read or reread some of those classic books or start out by reading a history that simply interests you. You may select a scholarly treatise on slave narratives or a breezy young adult book about Black pioneers. You will become acquainted with them because they are referenced over and over in most mainstream publications. At some point in your research you may need those specific sources for guidance and referral. Read something that spurs you on in your quest. Following is a sampling of the interesting subjects and resources out there for you to examine.

Andrews, William L. *To Tell a Free Story: The First Century of Afro-American Autobiography, 1760-1865*. Urbana: University of Illinois Press, 1986.

Aptheker, Herbert. *Negro Slave Revolts in the United States, 1526-1860*. New York: International Publishers, 1939.

Ashley, Leonard. *What's In a Name?: Everything You Wanted to Know*. Baltimore: Genealogical Publishing Company, Inc., 1996.

Barncs, Marian E. *Black Texans: They Overcame*. Austin, TX: Sunbelt Media, 1996.

Bentley, Elizabeth Petty. *The Genealogist's Address Book*. 3d edition. Baltimore: Genealogical Publishing Co., Inc., 1995. A prominent author in the field of genealogy provides a sourcebook of available resources organized by national, state, ethnic, religious, and special resources. Contact information for government agencies, archives, and genealogical repositories are included in an easy-to-use directory format.

Blassingame, John W., ed. *Slave Testimony: Two Centuries of Letters, Speeches, Interviews, and Autobiographies*. Baton Rouge: Louisiana State University Press, 1977.

Blockson, Charles L. *Black Genealogy*. Baltimore: Black Classic Press, 1991. A wonderful historical narrative of documentary and anecdotal resources highlighting the challenges and joys of African-American genealogical research. This reprint of the pioneering edition enables more researchers to benefit from Blockson's insight and strategy.

Brignano, Russell C. *Black Americans in Autobiography: An Annotated Bibliography of Autobiographies and Autobiographical Books Written Since the Civil War*. Rev. and expanded ed. Durham, NC: Duke University Press, 1984.

Byers, Paula K., ed. *African American Genealogical Sourcebook*. Detroit: Gale Research, Inc., 1995. Destined to become a classic in genealogy resources, this easy-to-follow guide book has garnered the expertise of prominent historians and researchers and set them out to survey and report on the unique trials and triumphs for the African-American genealogy project.

Chuks-orji, Ogonna. *Names from Africa: Their Origin, Meaning and Pronunciation*. Chicago: Johnson Publishing Company, Inc., 1972. Elegant in its brevity, this compilation provides a list of male and female African names including their meaning, language, and country of origin.

Costanzo, Angelo. *Surprizing Narrative: Olaudah Equiano and the Beginnings of Black Autobiography*. New York: Greenwood Press, 1987.

Croom, Emily A. *The Genealogist's Companion and Sourcebook*. Cincinnati: Betterway Books, 1994. A remarkable achievement by Croom, this book shows the more experienced genealogist how to work beyond basic research sources and methods and delves into such diverse and challenging arenas as specialized collections. Includes exceptional chapters on African-American and Native-American resources.

————. *Unpuzzling Your Past: A Basic Guide to Genealogy*. 3d edition. Cincinnati: Betterway Books, 1995. Regarded by professionals and amateurs as one of the most comprehensive and easy-to-understand books on the subject of genealogy. Croom's books are filled with sample records, charts, letters, worksheets, and straightforward narrative. A must for the beginning genealogist.

Curtain, Philip D. *The Attractive Slave Trade: A Census*. Madison: The University of Wisconsin, 1969.

Diawara, Manthia. *Black British Cultural Studies: A Reader*. Chicago: University of Chicago Press, 1995. Provides an overview of the history, culture, and race relations of persons from the African British diaspora.

Drake, Paul. *In Search of Family History: A Starting Place*. Bowie, MD: Heritage Books, Inc., 1992. Drake gives the reader the benefit of his legal knowledge by decoding the language and significance of legal documents, certificates, and terminology. Recommended for those at the intermediate stages of research.

Dulaney, W. Marvin. *Black Police in America*. Bloomington: Indiana University Press, 1996. Although not a genealogical resource, this unique historical accounting of the Black presence in law enforcement since the mid-19th century is an example of how specialized studies can provide useful history and context for genealogy.

Equiano, Olaudah. *The Interesting Narrative of the Life of Olaudah Equiano, or Gustavas Vassa, The African*. New York: St. Martin's Press (originally published 1789). This is one of the earliest published autobiographies by a Black man in the United States. His account of a childhood as an African, enslavement, and freedom is indicative of the kind of perseverance, intelligence, grace, and pride many early ancestors had.

Estell, Kenneth. *African America: Portrait of a People*. Detroit, MI: Visible Ink Press, 1994. This book updates the *Negro Almanac* (3d edition, 1977) and *African-American Almanac* (6th edition, 1994) with a new emphasis on biography. History as affected and influenced by notable African-Americans is clearly and attractively laid out in this single-volume encyclopedia. Recommended reading for gaining or reviving an appreciation of Black achievement.

Gerzina, Gretchen H. *Black London: Life Before Emancipation.* New Brunswick, NJ: Rutgers University Press, 1995.

Goodwine, Marquetta L. *The Legacy of Ibo Landing: Gullah Roots of African-American Culture.* Atlanta: Clarity Press Inc., 1998.

Goss, Linda and Clay Goss, eds. *Jump Up and Say! A Collection of Black Storytelling.* New York: Simon and Schuster, 1995. A truly inspired collection of some of African-America's well known and lesser known raconteurs, artists, wits, and writers—folks with something to say.

Ham, Debra Newman, ed. *The African-American Mosaic: A Library of Congress Resource Guide for the Study of Black History and Culture.* Washington, DC: Library of Congress, 1993. The oldest national cultural institution in the United States and the largest repository of recorded knowledge in the world asked eight contributors to provide a survey of the Library of Congress holdings relevant to the history of Black Americans in the United States. This book is readily available in most large public and university libraries and should be examined before making a trip to the Library of Congress.

Howells, Cyndi, *Netting Your Ancestors.* Baltimore: Genealogical Publishing Company, Incorporated, 1997. The computer whiz Cyndi Howells brings together resources from around the world.

Katz, William Loren. *Black Indians: A Hidden Heritage.* New York: Atheneum, 1986. An historical documentation of people with duel ancestry and Blacks who have lived with Native Americans in the Americas.

———. *Black Women of the Old West.* New York: Atheneum, 1995. The life stories and achievements of Black activists, army wives, mail-order brides, businesswomen, and pioneers are recounted with loads of detail and illustrations.

Krause, Carol. *How Healthy Is Your Family Tree? A Complete Guide to Creating a Medical and Behavioral Family Tree.* New York: MacMillan/Collier, 1994. Advice on how to construct your medical family tree.

Law, Nova. *African-American Genealogy Workbook.* Birmingham, AL: Legacy Publishing Company, 1995. A very attractive compendium of how-to information, forms, maps, and charts.

Lewin Arthur. *Africa Is Not a Country . . . It's a Continent!* Milltown, NJ: Clarendon Publishing Company, 1990. An example book designed for youth but packed with valuable historical and factual nuggets of information.

Marsh, Carole. *Black "Jography": The Paths of our Black Pioneers.* Atlanta, GA: Gallopade Publishing Group, 1994. A simple guidebook to black history.

Mellon, John, ed. *Bullwhip Days: The Slaves Remember.* New York: Weidenfeld & Nicolson, 1988.

Miller, Randall M., ed. *Dictionary of Afro-American Slavery.* Westport, CT: Greenwood Publishing Group, 1988. A scholarly examination of the history of slavery in the United States.

Mintz, Steven, ed. *African American Voices: The Life Cycle of Slavery.* Saint James, NY: Brandywine Press, 1993.

Parish, Peter J. *Slavery: History and Historians.* New York: Harper & Row, 1989.

Rosenbluth, Vera. *Keeping Family Stories Alive: A Creative Guide to Taping Your Family Life and Lore.* Point Roberts, WA: Hartley & Marks, Inc., 1990. Focus is on providing tips on the nuances of recording oral family history.

Sandel, Edward. *Black Soldiers in the Colonial Militia: Documents from 1639 to 1780.* Amite, LA: Tabor-Lucas Publications, 1994. Before requesting documents from the U.S. Archives, examine this collection of source materials excerpted from the Archives so you know what is available.

Smith, John D. *Black Voices from Reconstruction 1865–1877.* Brookfield, CT: Millbrook Press, Inc., 1996.

Stampp, Kenneth M. *Records of Antebellum Southern Plantations from the Revolution through the Civil War.* Frederick, MD: University Publications of America, 1985. A series of microfilm reels that contain records of plantation journals, plantation books, account books, inventories, diaries, etc. Available in Family History Library collections, genealogical and university libraries, and accompanied by "A Guide to Records of Antebellum Southern Plantations from the Revolution through the Civil War."

Streets, David H. *Slave Genealogy: A Research Guide with Case Studies.* Bowie, MD: Heritage Books, 1986. Provides method and detailed analysis on how to approach and glean information about the slave from a variety of resources.

Suter, Patricia and Corinne P. Earnest. *Kids & Kin: The Family History Research Vacation That Involves Kids.* East Berlin, PA: Russell D. Earnest Associates, 1997.

Vlach, John Michael. *Back of the Big House: The Architecture of Plantation Slavery.* The Fred W. Morrison series in Southern studies. Chapel Hill: University of North Carolina Press, 1992.

Voelz, Peter Michael. *Slave & Soldier; The Military Impact of Blacks in the Colonial Americas.* New York: Garland, 1993.

Walton-Raji, Angela. *African-American Ancestors Among the Five Civilized Tribes.* Bowie, MD: Heritage Books Inc., 1993. The

African-American presence among the Cherokees, Chicasaws, Choctaws, Creeks, and the Seminoles is reviewed, including former slave testimonies.

Wilson, Ellen Gibson. *John Clarkson and the African Adventure*. London: Macmillan, 1980.

Wright, Raymond S. 3rd. *The Genealogist's Companion Handbook: Modern Methods for Researching Family History*. Chicago, IL: American Library Association, 1995. Benefit from the wisdom Wright has acquired as a genealogist's genealogist with two decades of experience at the Family History Library in Salt Lake City and his renown as an author and speaker.

Young, Tommie Morton. *Afro-American Genealogy Sourcebook*. New York & London: Garland Publishing, Inc., 1987. This is an exhaustive resource, describing in detail the types of materials used in African-American genealogical research with examples, locations, primary and secondary resources, and more. After a decade, Morton's sourcebook remains one of the most authoritative and useable compendiums of its kind.

INDEX

A

Abolitionist movement, 23
Adoptees, Internet information for, 116
Africa
  African kingdoms, 17–18
  Egypt, 11, 13, 18
  Ethiopia, 18
  family history information sources, listing
    of, 98–100
  languages, 60–61
  number of slaves taken from, 25
  slaves in Africa, 18–19
  travel services to, 120–121
African-American genealogy
  budget for, 127
  census records, inspection of, 45–55
  cost of genealogy, 15–16
  documentation, collection of, 32–33
  genealogical societies, 15
  general guidelines, 126–131
  and goal for research, 41, 43
  interviews, 30–39
  mixed race Blacks, 22–23
  name research, 56–61
  organizing data, 39
  pedigree chart, 29–30, 31
  personal significance of, 9–16
  planning project, 126–127
  slavery era documents, 20
  worksheets for, 132–134
  See also Information sources
African-American History Association, 15
  address/phone for, 28, 106
African-American Mosaic, Web site, 113
African-American Network Resources, Web
  site, 114
African-Americans
  African roots, 17–19
  in American Revolution, 57
  bibliography of resources on, 150–157
  in Civil War, 23
  family reunions, 122–125
  family stories, 10–11
  passing (as Whites), 22–23
  pride in history of, 11–12
  slavery, 17–25
  White ancestry of, 22–23
Afrigeneas, Web site, 110–111
Afro-American Historical and Genealogical
  Society, 15
  address/phone, 28, 106–107
Aksum, kingdom of, 18
American Revolution, surnames of African-
  American soldiers, 57
America Online, genealogy information, 117
Ancient era, African kingdoms, 11, 13, 18
Angola, 25
Ashanti, 18
Asia, family history information sources,
  100–101
Autobiographies, as information source, 65
Aztecs, 24

B

Benin, 18, 19
Bible, as information source, 32–33
Big Book, Web site, 119
Biographies, as information source, 64–65
Birth certificates, 46
Black Family Reunion Celebrations, 122
Black Sal (Sally Hemings), 22
Brazil, slavery in, 24
Business records, 58

C

Cabral, Pedro, 24
Canada, family history information sources,
  listing of, 101–102
Caribbean
  family history information sources, 102–103
  slavery in, 24–25
Caroon, Robert, 10

Catalog, library research, 64
Census records, 45–55
    examples (1790–1920), 48–55
    in genealogical collections, 46–47
    importance of, 47
    in libraries, 46
    privacy protection, 55
    separate reports on Black population, 47–48
    slave schedules, 48
    Soundex, 59–60
    worksheets, 132–149
Chambers of commerce, information from, 68
Chattel slavery, 19
    beginning in Americas, 24
Christine's Genealogy Web site, 111–112
Civil War, Blacks in, 23
Columbus, Christopher, 19, 24
CompuServe, genealogy information, 117
Computer information
    genealogy software, 110
    Internet, 107–117
    online services, 117–120
Cuba, 25
    family history information sources, 103
Cyndi's List of Genealogy Sites on the
        Internet, Web site, 115

D
Dahomey, 17, 18
Death records, 46
    databases of, 118
Delaney, Bessie and Sadie, 38
Directories, as information source, 65
Documents
    census records, 45–55
    from family members, 32–33, 128–129
    for interview information, 38–39
    for name research, 58–59
    primary sources, 32–33
    public records, 32, 39, 45–55
    secondary resources, 32–33
    slave information, 20, 23, 25, 61
    tertiary resources, 33
    vital statistics, 46
Dominican Republic, 24
Driving records, 58

E
Ecomiedas, 24
Egypt
    Black African kingdom, 11, 13, 18
    Black African origins, 11, 13
    family history information sources, listing
        of, 98–99
Elders, interviewing, 30, 32–34, 128
Emancipation Proclamation, 14
England, genealogy methods in, 8
Ethiopia, 11
    Black African kingdom, 18

Everton Publishers, Web site, 115–116

F
Family group record, 42
    worksheet, 135
Family History Library, 46, 61, 66–67, 129
    Family History Centers, 46–47
    genealogical information of, 66–67
    phone number for, 67
    Social Security records, 118
    Web site, 112–113
Family reunions, 122–125
    coordinator for, 122–123
    planning/implementation of, 123–125
Family secrets, handling of, 41
Four11, Web site, 119
France, family history information sources, 101
Free Black Heads of Families in the First Census
        of the United States, 47

G
Gambia, 25, 61
Garvey, Marcus, 23
Gazetters, as information source, 65
GEDCOM, 110
Genealogical societies
    for African-American genealogy, 15, 27–28,
        105–107
    international, listing by country, 98–103
    resource material from, 26–27
    specialized information from, 67
    state by state listing of, 70–91
Genealogists, professionals, 120
Genealogy
    meaning of, 7
    popularity of, 9
    See also African-American genealogy
Genealogy Lady, Web site, 115
Genealogy Resources on the Internet, Web
        site, 114–115
Genogram, medical information, 10
George Archer's NetGuide, Web site, 114
Ghana, 18, 25
Griot, 30
Guinea-Bisseau, 25

H
Haiti, 24, 25
Haizlip, Shirley Taylor, 23
Haley, Alex, 12–13
    search process of, 61
Ham, 17
Handwritten records, problems of, 57
Having Our Say (Bessie and Sadie Delaney), 38
Heirlooms, 61
Hemings, Sally, 22
Henderson Travel Services
    African destinations, 121
    Web site, 121

Hispania, family history information sources,
102–103
Historical societies, as information source,
67–68
Homepages, genealogical, 116–117

I
Illness, tracing medical information, 10
Indentured servants, in colonial America, 21
Indexes, library research, 65–66
Information sources
African-American related sources, 105–107
census records, 45–55
chambers of commerce, 68
Family History Library, 66–67
genealogical societies, state by state listing
of, 70–91
historical societies, 67–68
international sources, listing by country,
98–103
on Internet, 107–117
interviews, 30–39
library, 62–66
for name research, 56–61
online services, 117–120
regional information, 68
travel as, 120–121
International resources, listing by country,
98–103
Internet
adoptee information, 116
family history information sources, 109–117
travel services, 120–121
Interracial relations, mixed race Blacks, 22–23
Interviews, 30–39
documentary support for information,
38–39
migratory information, 44
of older family members, 30, 32–34
questions for, 34–38
recording interviews, 128
time span for, 38
transcribing interviews, 128

J
Jefferson, Thomas, 22
Juffure, 120

K
Khanga, Yelenga, 97
Kinte, Kunta, 61
Kush, 17

L
Liberia, founding of, 99
Library of Congress, 46
Web site on Blacks in America, 113
Library research, 62–66
autobiographies, 65

biographies, 64–65
catalog, 64
census information, 46
directories, 65
gazetters, 65
indexes, 65–66
librarian, assistance of, 63
Los Negros, 24

M
Mailing lists, Web sites, 116
Mali, 17
Matrilineal societies, 8
Mayans, 24
Medical information, genogram, 10
Mestizo, 24
Middle Passage, 19
Migratory information, 44
Miscegenation. See Mixed race Blacks
Mixed race Blacks, 22–23
current number of, 22
passing (as Whites), 22–23
slave/master relations, 22
Mormons, Family History Library, 66–67

N
Name research, 56–61
African words, 60
common slave surnames, 57
difficulties of, 56–57
information sources, 58–59
nicknames/pet names, 58
oral tradition, 56
Soundex, 59–60
spelling inconsistencies, 57–58
trace back to Africa, 60–61
National Archives, 46, 60
Web site, 113
National Council of Negro Women, 122
National Genealogical Society
address/phone, 27
Web site, 114
National Register of Historic Places, African-
American related sites, 120
Native Americans, 8
disease from Whites, 24
Newsgroups, genealogical, 116
NEXIS-Express, death records, 118
Nicknames, 58
Nigeria, 25
information sources in, 99
Norsemen, 8

O
Open Records for Adult Adoptees, Web site,
116
Oral tradition
African griot, 30
name research, 56

Organization of data, 39
    family group record, 42
    filing system, 130
    geographical groupings, 39–40
    record keeping tools, 128
Origin myths, elements of, 7

P

Passing, as Whites, 22–23
Patrilineal societies, 8
Pedigree chart, 29–30, 31
    worksheet, 133
Primary sources, types of, 32–33, 127
Privacy protection, census records, 55
Prodigy, genealogy information, 117
Public records, 32, 39, 45–55
    on Internet, 129
Puerto Rico, 25

Q

Queen of Sheba, 11, 17
Questions, for interview of elders, 34–38

R

Racism, creation by slave owners, 19
Reconstruction, 14, 23
Record keeping. *See* Organization of data
Relationship chart, worksheet, 137
Research Institute of African and African
    Diaspora Arts, address/phone, 107
Roots (Haley)
    positive influence of, 12–13
    search process, 60, 61
ROOTS-L, 116
Roots Web Genealogical Data Cooperative,
    Web site, 116
Russia, family history information sources, 101

S

San Salvador, 24
Secondary resources, types of, 32–33, 127
Selassie, Haile, 18
Senegal, 25
    information sources of, 100
Sierre Leone, 25
Simeon the Crimean, 17
Slavery, 12, 18–25, 61
    African slave trade, 18–19
    in American history, 19–23

ancient era, 18–19
Black slave owners, 13
in Caribbean, 24–25
chattel slavery, 19
common slave surnames, 57
documentation of slaves, 20, 23, 25
by Europeans, 19
and mixed race ancestry, 22–23
number shipped to North America, 25
slave/master sexual relations, 22
in South/Central America, 24–25
and war, 18
Slave schedules, census records, 48
Social Security numbers, searches for, 118
Software, GEDCOM, 110
Solomon (Biblical), 18
Songhay, 17
*Soul to Soul: The Story of a Black Russian
    American Family 1865–1992* (Khanga), 97
Soundex, 59–60
South America
    family history information sources, 102–103
    slavery in, 24–25
Sudan, 18
Surnames
    of African-American soldiers, 57
    common slave surnames, 57
Sweeter the Juice, The (Haizlip), 23
Switchboard, Web site, 119

T

Telephone directories, Web sites, 118–119
Tertiary resources, types of, 33, 127
Timbuktu, 17

U

United States
    early peoples of, 8
    immigrant groups, 8
    slavery, historical view, 19–23
Universal Negro Improvement Association, 23

V

Vikings, 8
Vital statistics, types of, 45–46

W

War, and slavery, 18
Woodson, Thomas, 22